Christmas, 1964

To Karl,
   Merry Christmas,
      Millard and Kit

THE OBJECTIVE SOCIETY

THE
OBJECTIVE
SOCIETY

by
EVERETT KNIGHT

Introduction by William Barrett

GEORGE BRAZILLER, INC.

NEW YORK, 1960

To my Mother and Father
and to George

CONTENTS

So at length, gentlemen, we have reached the conclusion that the best thing for us to do is to do nothing at all, but to sink into a state of contemplative inertia.

DOSTOIEVSKI

INTRODUCTION

THERE used to be a popular program on TV (it may still be running for all I know) on which couples were selected as proper mates for marriage by Univac. The machine was fed the objective data on thousands of people and then ground out the names of the lucky pair who were ideally suited to each other. The couple reappeared each week to report publicly on the progress of their courtship. In the end (and let us at least be thankful for small favors) it was left to the couple themselves to decide whether or not they would marry. The stage when the machine decides is evidently the next step. What was most appalling in this whole performance was the great spirit of cheerfulness and good fun with which both audience and lucky couple accepted this submission of the human to the mechanical. After all, the machine is objective, and therefore should know better than our mere subjective feelings whom we should or should not take in marriage.

This instance may be bizarre, but it is not so very unusual these days, and it should remind us how the craze for a bogus and mechanical "objectivity" permeates the whole of our culture from top to bottom. Apparently the individual is in a bad way in modern society, in our Western world as well as in the East, or there would not be so many recent books on the depersonalization of man in our time. Mr. Knight's is, to my mind, one of the most noteworthy efforts in this direction because he does not confine himself to mere external social observation but cuts toward the philosophical root of the matter. The author is a young intellectual with very much bounce, and he is not interested, like some other writers in this field, in coddling anyone or anything involved in our present troubled situation. His tone is energetic, belligerent; and he sprays his shots in all directions. Not all of these hit the target, and it would be a rare reader who would not be provoked into disagreement by some of Mr. Knight's opinions, which range over a very wide gamut. Nevertheless, in its central contention this book seems to me right on target, and what it has to say should be a significant challenge to a good many Americans, particularly to some of our intellectuals.

How are we to understand ourselves and our time? For the existential thinker, and Mr. Knight is one, this is the pressing and central problem for philosophy, and not the search for an eternal realm of essences on which this world of appearance may be founded. But to understand our age is not something we shall arrive at by mere sociological compilations of data, for in that way we are led into too many peripheral matters which in the end only obscure our vision. The task of the existential thinker is to try to lay hold of what is central to his time. The truth—as Mr. Knight suggests, echoing the philosophers Husserl and Heidegger—is what is evident, what lies open and accessible to all, and not some little secret hidden behind the appearances of things. Of course, it takes considerable intelligence and wisdom to see what is before our eyes; it is in fact just what most of us miss seeing because our vision squints at little corners of facts here and there and we lose the large and enveloping scene altogether. Hence, the truth, which is precisely what is open and evident, is also what is concealed. Long ago the philosopher Berkeley observed that men complain that they cannot see when they have first kicked up a dust before their own eyes.

Now, the dominating force of our age is Mathematical Physics, along with the technology that ensues from this. Nothing shows this more clearly than the threat of the H-bomb and intercontinental rockets—a stage of history when the contest between the two greatest powers, America and Russia, has become a contest between their mathematical physicists. Mathematical physics, of course, is the triumph of objectivity moving in the domain of the quantitative and the measurable.

Or, again, this crisis of our time is just as plainly dramatized for us in the emergence of the space age itself: at the moment when man stands at the threshold of being able to launch himself into space, he leaves this old planet behind him in a worse human tangle than ever. Our crisis lies in this discrepancy between man's vast technological power over the world of objects and his woeful inadequacy as yet to deal with the human condition. Man himself lags behind his own works. While his power to deal with the world of matter has multiplied enormously, his wisdom in coping with the world of the human spirit seems to be exactly where it was, or perhaps even worse. No wonder it is tempting for some minds, intoxicated by the prodigies and miracles of mathematical physics, to attempt to turn the same passion for "objectivity," for the quantitative and measurable, to the domain of the human expecting the same prodigies and miracles there. The attempt, of course, merely sinks us deeper in the mire of this age of objects.

What I have observed here is, of course, no secret, and many humanists have repeatedly insisted upon it as *the* problem of our time. Where Mr. Knight's book seems to me to go beyond most of these complaints is in calling attention to the fact that a certain tradition of Classical Rationalism, almost endemic to Western culture, lies behind this situation and is at once both our triumph and our trouble. Let us remember that it is the Frenchman Descartes who is usually taken as having ushered in the modern era of thought in the seventeenth century. And what is philosophy to Descartes except a means of clearing the way to the mathematical conception of nature and the possibility of mathematical physics? Descartes is commonly taken as the initiator of modern thought because he exemplifies the spirit of reason and free inquiry; actually, his famous sceptical doubts already appear in St. Augustine, and in the central features of his philosophy Descartes remains within the womb of the Middle Ages. What really emerges as new and historically decisive with Descartes is his mathematical conception of nature: the very essence of a material object is extension—that is, the quantitative and measurable dimensions of the thing—this and nothing else. Here the seed of what Mr. Knight castigates as "the objective mind"—that is, the mental attitude that hopes to reduce all things in nature to the quantitative and measurable—is first dropped into the fertile soil of Western thought, and now in our time, three centuries after Descartes, this seed has come to fruit in all those marvelous prodigies of mathematical physics that, unfortunately, also happen to threaten our lives. Clearly, the thoughts of philosophers can be fateful steps in the history of mankind.

This passion to reduce everything to the quantitative and measurable is not, however, the only way in which the spirit of objectivity operates in the modern mind: there is also the detachment, the unwillingness to take sides, to be, as one says, "truly objective," that one finds among scholars and intellectuals. The scholar is supposed to be an objective researcher; that is his calling. All this seems very admirable on the surface, but when pushed to an extreme it results in nothing less than intellectual castration. Thus the literary scholar is supposed to expound the text without necessarily having any aesthetic judgment of his own, much less aesthetic passion: and he ends by losing any capacity for creative taste altogether.

To some intellectuals Mr. Knight's attack (chiefly in Chapter Two) on the academic mind for its passionless objectivity will seem excessive, but from my own experience within the academic cloisters I do not find it so. After all, what is the point of all those years of scholarly study if at the end the scholar can only be objective and has not reached any conclusions of his own? One curious sign of the sad chaos in our universities right now is that while philosophy departments come under the division of the Humanities, nevertheless in the prevailing climate of opinion here, the philosophers hold that the only valid knowledge is that of science. At best the philosophers will accord to their humanist colleagues knowledge of facts— the dates of Shakespearean editions or the "objective" facts about Elizabethan England—but the real thing that would ever justify us in saying that a man *knows* his Shakespeare, namely the ability to see Shakespeare's plays aesthetically and imaginatively—for this the philosopher has no recognition nor room in his system; he does not even have at his disposal the concepts by which to interpret that kind of knowledge. Yet he continues to rub elbows, smile and greet, and even have luncheon with his humanist colleagues. A small and merely intramural affair, the reader may think; but not at all, for the academic world here truly holds the mirror up to the larger world, where the quantitative and the objective are taken as the norms of all knowledge.

The sources of Mr. Knight's thinking are French, and particularly the philosophy of Sartre. Considering the insularity of Anglo-American thought at the moment, I hardly find this continental influence a defect. Besides, Mr. Knight does not parrot Sartre, he brings the Sartrian mode of thought to bear on our American situation. With Sartre he understands that all thought is a human project, and therefore a mode of action on the part of man who is fundamentally a being enmeshed in the world. In the act of thinking itself the thinker is engaged in taking sides, or struggling toward taking sides. To be above the battle, or somehow outside it, is not thinking but rather savoring one's mental lollilop. Since the Cold War the spirit of objectivity has invaded our intellectuals in the form of a kind of tired indifference to politics. One sign of this is that no really important political writing has appeared in America or England during the last decade: a magazine like *Partisan Review* has virtually had to give up politics because most of its political articles are too stale or boring or irrelevant. But if thinking is involvement, then Mr. Knight's summons to rethink old political positions is very much to the point. I hope, in any case, that our intellectuals here will take it to heart.

WILLIAM BARRETT
New York City, 1960

THE OBJECTIVE SOCIETY

PREFACE

ALL of philosophy's 'radical' new departures are eventually seen to be in large part illusory. We cannot bring *everything* into question without ceasing to be of a given time and place. Thus, classical rationalism is founded upon faith in a universe functioning as a mechanism, and therefore in a manner perfectly intelligible to man. But if such is the nature of our world then why should not men long before the renaissance have had more knowledge of how it works? The answer given was that ancient and medieval philosophy had failed to make a clear distinction between the subjective and the objective—only what is measurable is objective, the so-called secondary qualities belong to the perceiving subject. In this way the initial and arbitrary assumption of intelligibility led to the postulation of an 'inner world' consisting of two parts: the intellect, knifing its way to the bone of Reality, and subjectivity, irrelevant or even harmful to the pursuit of truth.

There are probably few people today who will object to the view that science is not the discovery of Reality, as the nineteenth century supposed, but of a given aspect of reality; it is, in other words, a description and not an explanation. But if we go this far, if science is not concerned with 'ultimate' truth and is consequently (apart from its value as a tool) a metaphysics like any other, then it is time we reformed our ideas about intellect and subjectivity. If scientific law is no longer to be regarded as exhaustive and final, but simply as one of many ways in which matter has been and can be organized, then what is primordial in man is not intellect, but that 'intention' or

1

'orientation' which intellect helps him to exploit. Initially at least, scientific or philosophical problems are not given. We create them by striving to achieve this or that; they have no existence outside the framework of specific cultural orientations. But this is not all. It is the 'intentions' that we hold in common with most of our fellows that constitute the identity of objects. Much of the thinking of G. E. Moore on the subject of perception consists in wondering how common sense can be so sure that a chair is a chair and that it actually exists, despite the many excellent reasons philosophers have given us for believing some quite different things. For example, in *Some Main Problems of Philosophy* (the chapter entitled 'Sense Data'), Moore asks how a group of people can recognize an object as an envelope even though the sense data perceived by each might differ radically. He concludes that 'There must . . . be some other ways of knowing of the existence of things besides the mere direct apprehension of sense data and images' (p. 49). This is a notion he returns to repeatedly (on pages 73 and 119, for example). In *Philosophical Studies* he takes matters a step further (in the chapter 'Some Judgements of Perception') by suggesting that we do not perceive sense data, we perceive objects; or, as he puts it: '. . . this presented object . . . is identical with this part of the surface of this inkstand' (p. 247). It was inevitable for Moore to fear that this view might be what he calls sheer nonsense—for it to be anything else he would have had to do what Husserl was doing at that time in Germany, he would have had to scrap classical epistemology almost in its entirety and start out afresh. 'We are all', writes Moore in "A Defence of Common Sense", 'in this *strange* position; that we know many things . . . and yet we do not know *how* we know them.' We know them because we 'intend' them. How this can be is something we shall consider as we go along. All I wish to do now is explain the way in which the word 'subjectivity' will be used in this book. It is 'intention' and not thing (hence Sartre will call it a 'nothingness'), it is a simple 'turning toward'; and if this is so, then there is no complex inner machinery of recognition, there is only the object of which there is consciousness.[1] We are conscious of the envelope and

---

[1] Moore comes very close to this conception. In 'The Refutation of Idealism' he writes: '. . . the moment we try to fix our attention upon consciousness and to see *what*, distinctly, it is, it seems to vanish.' Or again: 'When we try to introspect the sensation of blue, all we can see is the blue. . . .' etc. Nevertheless Moore felt that consciousness must be perceptible in some way; positing it as a 'nothingness' would have involved an impossibly radical break with the past.

not of varying sense data unless, as the result of a change of intention, we wish to perceive sense data. What I want to emphasize in particular, however, is that this conception of subjectivity supplants the whole of the 'inner world' to which occidental thought has given birth during the past four centuries. The self, for example, is not a 'thing' either; it is the most sustained, deeply-rooted and carefully concealed of our intentions. This being the case, such terms as 'introspection' and 'self-awareness' are meaningless in their generally accepted sense. A self considered as a fixed entity would have to be artificially created and maintained; and this of course is, in many people, the function of introspection which is an interminable and abortive activity precisely because the self is act and not object.

We are about to enter an age of space travel entertaining ideas which have come down to us from antiquity. But should it not occur to us that what might be needed is a change of cultural orientation upon which idea depends, and which thought is in some measure powerless to produce? Such reorientations first manifest themselves in art or literature, and if we look for some movement in the arts which diverges from the past as strikingly as science has caused our way of life to diverge from that of our forefathers, we can hardly avoid coming upon cubism. We see now that the work of artists like Giotto and Uccello was of the highest philosophical as well as artistic significance. We see that there is a clear affinity between Uccello's perspective and Galileo's law of inertia. An experimental verification of this law would have strengthened Galileo's hand, but the work of Uccello offered the most precious of all support; it guaranteed that enquiry was orientating itself in Galileo's direction. No amount of successful experimenting will make men see what they do not wish to see. Modern art appears to me to lend invaluable support to those developments of modern thought from which this book derives and to nullify others. This is the reason for my frequent references to it.

The art, literature and philosophy of our time are beginning to cause occidental culture as it has existed since the renaissance to appear alien. We can fight this alienation if we wish, and that is what Anglo-Saxon thinkers are doing by refusing to be interested in a proposition vital to the best continental philosophy since Husserl, and which I have just mentioned; namely, that man is not a product (that is, a thing), he is that orientation which gives rise periodically

3

to new cultures which are at once so alike and so profoundly different.

It has become apparent to all that the study of humanity cannot be usefully pursued if we continue to regard causality, even after physics itself has partially abandoned it, as a legitimate explanation. An act does not have a cause in the classical sense of the word; it has an intention, a purpose. The purpose may be exceedingly obscure, even to the person who entertains it, hence the need for psycho-analysis. On the social level also, there is no explanation apart from considerations of purpose, and it is this conviction on my part which largely accounts for what some readers may consider to be unfair or unsound methods of dealing with the subject.

It accounts for the indignation, since if we are not mere products of our society and environment, or of God, if, on the contrary, we 'intend' these phenomena in a way which I hope will become clearer later on, then we (and above all we who are teachers) are responsible for the intellectual bankruptcy of the present-day Anglo-Saxon world.

It accounts for the nature of the argument, which is in reality an attempt to characterize a given mentality by enquiring into the tasks it has set itself. What I am attacking is not a philosophical position, but a philosophical attitude. This is something which lies beyond the scope of persuasion by argument. There is no possibility of agree-ment between two men who are 'orientated' in different ways. Thus my assertion that our culture is now bankrupt is not of a sort that one proves. What is, depends upon what one wants; and for reasons we will discuss, the objective society is condemned by its own logic to want the stagnation of the 'free world'. Its purpose is to be with-out a purpose. This may be verified simply by remarking that the term 'polemical' is a dirty word among academics and most critics. Or again, if we ask a teacher of philosophy, for example, what he is contributing to his society (and such a question is apt to be regarded as an impertinence) he may well reply that it is his modest purpose to teach his students to think clearly. The philosopher devoted to clear thought, however, is like the man who keeps his car in excellent running order without ever going anywhere in it. He may be com-pared to the writer whose one interest is style and who therefore has nothing to tell us. This is putting matters at best, since there is nothing to prevent clear thinking from being directed to evil ends. We are far removed from philosophy as 'the bad conscience of its

4

age'—aggressive, irreverent and exhilarating, striving to answer our perplexities and to point the way. Such thinking is not primarily clear, it is primarily forceful, because it has an overriding purpose; it will become clear when its purpose is eventually achieved.

I

Western society is adrift. Its relative material prosperity causes
us to overlook its ideological emptiness, an emptiness that much
more surprising in that it co-exists with a colossal apparatus of learning. Erudition is not intelligence to be sure, but need there be an
antipathy? Just what is the function of non-scientific learning, since
we can no longer keep up the fiction that all learning should be
scientific? Is its function to be objective? It would appear so since
objectivity is our conscience and our morality. It has its priesthood
—the intellectuals—who lead lives of exemplary aloofness from the
squabbles of the day, and who are not far from seeing in such critical
detachment our one hope of access to a better life. We are on hallowed
ground here, for the Greeks—and who does not admire the Greeks?
—saw that emotion is disruptive of orderly living and that it should
be controlled by the judgement. There is more in objectivity than
this, as there is more in christianity than in the pagan religions;
'more' in the sense that christianity introduces a *historical* past and
a foreseeable future. The wisdom of the ancients was to have concentrated upon living, that of christianity to have avoided living—
the first requires intelligence, the second erudition; the philosopher
is replaced by the monk. To which of the two are we to compare the
academic intellectual?

There are troubled times when the monk must man his walls
against the Norseman or the Mongol. He does it badly because it is
not his business to survive, but to be right. If it were a mere question

7

of survival, then during the thirties nothing could have been more natural for us than to seek the help of the communists against the fascists who were offering the most immediate threat to our way of life. And yet the intellectuals who committed themselves to communism have ever since been offering unsolicited auto-criticisms. In many cases, their concern was, in reality, not only to combat fascism, but to be right; and communism gradually showed itself to be just another political system rather than the Truth finally revealed. The common man's absorption in matters directly concerned with his material well-being is no more reprehensible than the intellectual's pursuit of spiritual comfort. There is a modesty in the wish for a car or for better food and drink that is lacking in the wish to know the Answer; the revolt of the workers is preferable to the elegant sulking of the intellectual deprived of an Absolute. The hunger for food may be satisfied, not that for the Truth, because there is none; and it is probable that the real revolution of our time is the discovery that while something can be done about hunger, nothing can be done about spiritual hunger. This is what the intellectuals failed to understand. They thought marxism was a religion; but it is simply, in its present form, the answer to hunger, and they are better advised to turn to catholicism as many of them have.

Our error during the thirties was to have given in to the primitive lust to believe; but one is more commonly made to understand that the real lesson of those difficult times is that the intellectual does not sin against objectivity without betraying his mission. Partisanship is the enemy, and we must steel ourselves against the siren calls of practical utility, against the naïve belief that erudition is there to serve a purpose.

It would be comforting to be able to thrust politics out of our lives altogether, as one might have done a century ago; but it is by politics that we shall live or die, and yet all we have found to oppose to the vulgar successes of marxism in some of the most populous parts of the world is 'pluralism'; that is, objectivity disguised as a political philosophy. This gives us some idea both of the importance to be attributed to the notion of objectivity in our society, and the need there is for us to be clear about its real nature; for objectivity strictly adhered to necessarily involves passivity. In the case of pluralism, government is envisaged not only as representing diverse groups, but as impartially arbitrating their differences. But such a government can only recommend; if it attempts to implement a decision it becomes a partisan, it ceases to conduct itself objectively toward the plurality of interests to which it gives voice. Pluralism is the nostalgic idealization of a system hardly less sordid than any other, and one which, into the bargain, could not possibly operate, because absolute governmental impartiality would mean governmental paralysis. The hypocrisy we associate with nineteenth-century British capitalism is an essential element of the system. Michel Leiris calls the royalism of his adolescence an 'imaginary refuge', and 'a means of turning away from the real'. There is this in pluralism as there is in most conservatism. The 'irreality' of pluralism—since government either takes sides as in the welfare state, or remains a tool in the hands of a financial oligarchy, not to mention its total inapplicability in most other parts of the world at a time when the necessity for global thinking should be self-evident[1]—its disembodied purity, reminiscent of the clean-handed communism of the thirties, mark it as a product of the intellectuals.

Is it not alarming that in a century as political as ours, political thinking in Anglo-Saxon countries should have ceased to exist? An intellectual not interested in politics is like a seventeenth-century schoolman not interested in science. Our intelligentsia is another third estate; it is nothing and should be everything. But unlike the old third estate, ours accepts its nothingness, it does not appear to it incredible that the brains of a society should actually trail behind the mass of the people; and this is what happens when the intellectual converts himself to religion or mysticism, or when he eagerly seizes upon any evidence that stalinism might be, just as he thought, the whole of communism. The dislike with which a good many intellectuals consider the possibility of a genuinely humane communism bears a sinister resemblance to what American business called the 'peace scare' which resulted from talk about a negotiated peace in Korea.

Since the Anglo-Saxon intellectual, unlike his French counterpart, is usually an academic, he is, as we have remarked, an erudite rather than a thinker. Thinking is a positive activity, its function is to enable us to adapt ourselves with the least delay and the greatest effectiveness to new situations. In theory, information has much to do with this process; but if this is the case why do we take it for granted that the learned man will be almost invariably no more than

[1] If pluralism does not wish to lay claim to universality (as at one time it would not have hesitated to do) then it is not a political philosophy at all.

a spectator. The information of the intellectual allows him to appreciate that he is living through two of the most considerable events of human history—the Russian and Chinese revolutions; yet this fact coexists with an almost total neglect, not to say contempt, of marxism throughout the English-speaking world. Not that the Chinese example has much of a practical nature to teach us; on the contrary, China has been awakened by a political philosophy that after all is ours, and she will accomplish her immense task of rehabilitation thanks to a science that is ours. One grows desperately tired of hearing even the well educated (especially the well educated) use the expression 'the free world' to cover the simple fact that part of the world is moved by the enthusiasm that saves, while the rest of it no longer knows which way to turn, but is delighted that it should still be free not to turn at all. What I have called enthusiasm, however, others are quick to call fanaticism, so ready are we to attribute our vices to others. For *les extrêmes se touchent*, the fanaticism of the illiterate is but the other face of the intellectual's need for the spiritual comfort of final answers. The hideous intolerance of the Church has few if any parallels in the history of China (or in antiquity). What communism should be teaching us now is not the inevitable association of accomplishment and fanaticism, but that any answer to our problems must be expressed in political terms. Our task is to revive political enthusiasm without the fanaticism. But one of the roots of fanaticism is the false notion that an act depends for its effectiveness upon the soundness of the idea which preceded it. This was the error of eighteenth- and nineteenth-century political rationalism. In reality the idea grows out of the act or is co-extensive with it, just as applied science (which had previously been 'philosophy') grew out of the industrial revolution. The historian justifies or rationalizes the act from which there was no turning back, like the execution of Louis XVI, and imagines he has discovered part of what 'lay behind' the revolution. But history is an act of passion, and the world was to bear little resemblance to what the rationalists had wished it to be.[1] The truth is neither revealed nor discovered, it is created. What therefore is to become of the intellectual who has

[1] Written constitutions (with the exception of the American which is now, however, in desperate need of revision) bring little satisfaction to the countries for which they were elaborated, while governments which have evolved uninterruptedly through the centuries seem to function more smoothly. The instability of French government is not unconnected with the French fondness for ideas. The Englishman's success at compromise is one aspect of his dislike of ideas.

10

always considered it his function either to plan the ideal society or to withdraw into a protective contemplation of a 'cultural heritage', when it is seen that effective thought is inseparable from act, and when our problems for the moment are political not cultural, social and not individual?

The ills of a society are the ills of those whose business it is to do its thinking. Our intellectuals have not only ceased to think, they consider it their duty not to think—their function being to compile facts out of which will emerge the Truth by immaculate conception.

We can therefore talk, I think, of a double betrayal, for we have identified two types of intellectual—the messiah and the monk. The great century of the intellectual with a mission was, of course, the last; and what is remarkable about him now is his self-effacement, the messianic impulse having subsided into an occasional conversion, or, after having turned to communism for a while has now in many cases become a virulent anti-communism. The messianic intellectual (Koestler is a good example), like the believer, needs a world in which Right and Wrong are clean-contoured and clearly labelled. Communism having been wholly good is now wholly evil, like the fallen angel. Between those offering single and timeless answers to the many and changing questions with which the day confronts us, and those who have fallen asleep over their interminable compilations, between these two we can come to no good. By thinking abstractly or by refusing to think at all, the intellectuals have ceased to count. This was not always so, and it is important that we try to understand how it has come about. The Englishman above all should be concerned here for one has the impression that only in this country (America perhaps not excepted, for there the intellectual no longer speaks his whole mind) are the intellectuals as a majority if not conservative[1] at least indifferent (which comes to the same thing), and conservatism is whatever one wishes, but it is certainly not thought considered as a constructive activity.

If we give to objectivity its broadest definition—faith in the existence of an 'Object' (God, scientific or historical 'law', the Nation, etc.), independent of our subjective appreciation—then the messianic urge is clearly objective in nature. To be sure, it is pre-

[1] The Englishman who has passed through the public schools and Oxford or Cambridge has received more an indoctrination than an education. The political opinions of the British working man are apt to be sound more often than those of the intellectual. In America the reverse is true.

11

cisely for his lack of objectivity that this type of intellectual is ordinarily condemned; nevertheless the difference between him and his more 'objective' brothers is one of method, not of kind; the issue being to decide upon an attitude toward the Object, and not to enquire whether it really exists. We are all nationalists, some of us more objectively than others. Depending upon temperament or historical circumstance one will be content to contemplate the Object or one will seek to co-operate with it. Monasteries are shaken by the winds of reform, or faith in perfectibility through science and reason is supplanted by marxism, the socialist by the communist revolutionary. Perhaps I am only restating in different form the old belief that men are of two kinds—platonists or aristotelians, idealists or empiricists, mathematicians or experimentalists. But here again the difference is one of method—the platonist begins with the Idea, the aristotelian makes it the goal of his investigations; neither doubts its existence. Whether it is mind or things which contribute most to meaning, meaning is there and it is exhaustive. The monk and the reformer, the rationalist and the revolutionary, the idealist and the empiricist all 'contemplate' or worship, one passively the other actively, like the regular and secular clergy of old.

The despair which is the occupational disease of modern intellectuals grows out of their double inability to believe in Objects and to function without them. These are the 'hollow men' with whom it is difficult to sympathize because one senses that they savour their despair as the romantic savoured his melancholy. But to the extent in which disillusionment is a necessary step toward the 'other side of despair', to use Sartre's phrase, it is to be preferred to the artificial paradise of the believer. Science has ceased to imagine itself on the way to definitive results, and it is no doubt this in part which explains the disorientation of the intellectual. But the advent of the absurd in no way disquiets the academic who, with his eyes as usual resolutely fixed upon the past, has taken to denouncing political rationalists from Plato to Marx for their 'naïve' belief in the existence of political solutions. All our troubles it is argued stem from the messianic mentality, from the 'possessed' as Dostoievski calls them, one of whom he causes to remark: 'I began with absolute freedom and I have ended with a despotism equally absolute.'[1] It is well that this

---

[1] But could the Russians have faced up to the colossal task before them without being 'possessed'? Had the Dostoievskis prevailed the master race would not have been stopped at Stalingrad.

should have been discovered (belatedly, it is true, but presumably the necessity of 'historical perspective' requires that the academic arrive upon the scene several generations after it is too late to be of any use to the artist or the thinker) but the question now is how long is it going to take us to see that to condemn the messiah is at the same time to condemn his blood brother, the monk? If there are no moral, scientific or political Absolutes, then it is as pointless to go on 'contemplating' them as it is to try to attain them; as useless to preserve them as to try to implement them, the Truth is no more in the past than in the future. The great liberation, brought about not only by the 'death of God' but of Absolutes whatever their nature, has not been joyfully received; quite the contrary, because the 'eternal Truths' are not discovered, they are created to shield us against the absurd. They are a Father Christmas for adults. Furthermore, if there is no Object to propitiate or obey, then *we* are fully responsible for what goes on among us; but the responsibility of the intellectual which is the heaviest of all he eschews by talk of objectivity. In the life of both the messiah and the monk, the Object plays much the same role—that of a refuge against the solitude of meaninglessness and responsibility. How then did the objectivity of one come to be considered the antithesis of that of the other?

Objectivity in the sense of impartiality is of course a product of science, and if objectivity is the morality of the intellectual it is because for several centuries science has been his religion.

The religion of the middle ages was more than a creed, more than a faith, it was a *perception*; not that human vision has changed in the past seven or eight hundred years, what has changed are those aspects of the exterior world which we choose to emphasize. For example, we see objects neither in perspective (since a person in the distance is seen at his true height and not as a dwarf) as orthodox art would have it, nor without depth (since we see objects to be at a greater or lesser distance from us) as the medieval artist depicted them. We must not imagine perspective to be a device the discovery of which enabled artists to picture things as they 'really are'; it was a new kind of perception, and one which would naturally accompany the change from the 'closed' aristotelian-christian world where all of space was accounted for to the 'open' or infinite world of mathematics and geometry where, according to Galileo, objects once in motion would, under ideal conditions, move for ever in

13

straight lines—like those that children are taught to rule upon paper in order to give depth to the scene they are representing. The world is unchanging, yet in a very real sense there is more than one. We see what we expect to see, not what is 'really there'. A person hears an explosion, sees someone fall and is prepared to swear he saw a revolver, although there was none. In this case something was seen that did not exist; but the demon-ridden world of the romanesque churches did exist, only the 'diabolical' face we quickly forget was once an incarnation smelling of sulphur. A given vision of the world systematically neglects whatever cannot be made to fit and invents whatever is necessary to fill in the vacant spaces; and so a characteristic perception comes into being which other generations will find all but impossible to enter into.

It is in this sense that we are no longer religious. True religion is a perception—we may talk of God and the devil, but we no longer see them, our vision is no longer orientated in their direction. Medieval perception made unbelief impossible; scientific perception makes belief impossible. The collapse of science as a metaphysic has not yet altered our perception, and Aquinas can never be brought back except to the universities. One of Husserl's 'regions of being' may well be assigned to religious sentiment, but it will be one exploited by very few, and a philosophical justification is a poor substitute for the practical accomplishment of which the religion of the middle ages was capable. Or have we ceased to be interested in practical accomplishment? Or more exactly perhaps, do we fancy ourselves as having accomplished all that is possible, like Cyril Connolly's Palinurus? But it is precisely our helmsmen—our alleged thinkers—who are accomplishing nothing at all.

One is tempted to simplify Comte's famous divisions of history and to look upon all human thought as an anthropomorphism, religious or scientific. Not until almost the present century when it began to appear that the universe and mind might be foreign to one another, so that the non-human could only be described as absurd, not until the advent of this first genuine atheism can we consider thought as having undergone a radical change of direction. The 'dehumanization' of the world of which it is customary to complain is the effect of the disappearance of the gods, for gods are other men with enviable powers. Man has always deified himself; and while the rationalists knew that if triangles had gods they would be triangular, their god, though of no particular appearance, was

14

rational. It would appear possible to talk here of a continuous withdrawal, in the sense of an increasing abstraction, from the days when gods walked among men as Pharaoh, as the Roman Emperor or as Christ, through the middle ages when (after having become One, or at most Three) He appeared in person only to the mystics, to the implacable robot god of celestial mechanics and predestination. The renaissance did not bring atheism, but on the contrary a great intensification of religious feeling with protestantism; and a purification of it in the case of the humanists who, including Rabelais, were anticlericals, not atheists. The great thinkers of the sixteenth and seventeenth centuries were not, for either themselves or their contemporaries, the fathers of modern science, they were neo-theologians, concerned not with the nature of God as had been the scholastics, but with the way in which he performed his wonders. The alarm of the Church was, none the less, fully justified. God was becoming more remote. It was no longer he himself who was accessible to his creatures, but only the way in which his great work functioned. When it was discovered that the sun and stars are made of stuff familiar to us and not of an entirely unworldly substance as Aristotle had supposed, common clay filled the visible universe, and the whole heavenly apparatus disappeared for good; disappeared, that is, in the sense that it was no longer perceived; a fact perhaps not unconnected with the protestant repugnance for art in religion, especially inasmuch as it was the protestant countries which were the most receptive to the new science. In Italy, Michelangelo brings to an end the renaissance in art not only because technically it could be carried no further but because his merciless Christ of the Sistine Chapel suggests the existence of a law which God himself might be powerless to change. Art would be less and less preoccupied with the sacred because the sacred was ceasing to be human; it was ceasing to be perceived. It could only be thought.

Medieval perception accepted uncritically the evidence of the senses, scientific perception is based upon mistrust of them. The first law of the scientific attitude is not to believe what one sees; the truth is never in appearances; and Galileo himself was aware that the new philosophy marked a return to Plato.[1] We associate very closely in

[1] Modern philosophy has been little more than epistemology because it accepted this all-important notion that appearance must be 'corrected' by the judgement. The rebirth of philosophy in phenomenology and existentialism was brought about by the repudiation of the scientific conception of truth as hidden behind appearance.

our minds science and experiment; but, in its origins, science was not experimental—it was Francis Bacon's error to have supposed that it could be. Experiment cannot even know where to begin without the scaffolding of theory and hypothesis. The function of the experiment is to verify or to eliminate a supposition; it seldom discovers, except by accident. Thus Galileo was not led to the law of inertia through a series of experiments; he conceived the law and knew that an experiment, even had one been possible, would have been superfluous. It is the aristotelian who, in one of Galileo's dialogues, asks whether an experiment had been made, to which Galileo replies that none was necessary.

The mind is the laboratory of science, and it is the traditional concept of mind as the interpreter of sense impressions coming to it from without which has formed what I have called our scientific perception. It seems to us a truth as old as Aesop that the senses deceive, yet in general they were not considered to do so before the sixteenth or seventeenth centuries. The qualities of things were a perfectly reliable indication of their nature. Heat or cold were not inessential changes that substances were liable to undergo, but part of the nature of objects, and the means by which they were identified. For us, earth and air *are* whatever chemical analysis reveals them to be; for antiquity and the middle ages, earth was dry, air was light. Things 'contained' their qualities as bodies contained souls. There was an attempt made toward the end of the middle ages to explain motion by an 'impetus' implanted in the moving object. Science is platonic not only because it is number, but because it was a great stride toward the identification of the 'essences' which are the ultimate reality and which things both manifest and conceal. These essences, or laws, were, of course, conceived as universal and objective, and since measurement is both these things, it was clearly indispensable to rid objects of whatever qualities could not be measured. One cannot measure colour or smell, nor 'impetus' considered as something 'in' the object; and so there came into being the famous distinction between primary and secondary qualities. For the medieval mind, the ability to cause a tickling sensation was a 'virtue' residing in feathers, and not a susceptibility residing in the person. Just as science was removing God from our field of vision, it was removing man himself from the things about him with which he had conversed so intimately that one thinks of the 'participation' that Lévy-Bruhl attributes to the primitive mentality. The renaissance

16

was the beginning of an immense 'alienation' that was to leave man more and more abandoned to his own resources, and this gradual suppression of the sacred and of the supernatural is an important source of the individualism we associate with the renaissance and which the humanist has made the basis of his ethic. In protestantism the individual becomes his own priest; the greater awfulness of God which was a consequence of the incalculable increase in the vastness of the universe provoked a feeling of greater personal responsibility, the result being a weaker religion, but stronger individuals. The truth which had disappeared from appearances had to a considerable extent taken refuge in the mind; for there were now two worlds, the 'inner' and the 'outer' which, for several centuries to come, philosophy was to try to put together. The God of the protestants had become more ruthless, and more enigmatically so, than the Jehova of the Hebrews; but in a godless world, man had to aid him an infallible conscience. Similarly, if man's reassuring commerce with things had been interrupted it was to accede to a single universal Principle through mind. This communion between the subject and the object, between the individual and the Absolute, was to dominate our culture to the present day.

In the protestant and the humanist (broadly considered as the most informed man of his time), we have the first modern appearance of the messiah and the monk. They were the products of the great scission between the creator and his creation which was to widen as the centuries went by. For while in the middle ages the world was symbolic of God or even part of God like the bread and wine of communion, early science was to see in it merely the purpose or plan of God. It was becoming possible to turn one's thoughts to what was not God, to what was neither good nor evil; and the witchcraft persecutions of the seventeenth century were one of the last manifestations of a mentality for which good and evil were in things as well as in thoughts. It was becoming necessary to interpret a world (or 'to justify the ways of God to man') which it had once been sufficient to look at to understand. If logic was the science of the middle ages, it was because words expressed things with the same fullness with which a mathematical symbol expresses a quantity. But now thoughts (i.e. language) could no longer be exercised upon things themselves which were an agglomeration of secondary qualities; and even when the identity of the object had been established, it could not be meaningful in itself, but only as a manifestation of the law governing objects of this kind.

17

The breakdown of medieval unity into God *and* the world, along with the transformation of perception into something interior, gave rise to the problem as to whether this interior perception communicated with God (conscience), or only with His Order (intellection). Both Montaigne and Pascal deny that God may be attained through reason—this view being left to the Church which had begun the fossilization to which it owes its survival—and these two men represent in their noblest forms the contemplative and the messianic cast of mind and personality. For the first, the creation is enough; for the second, there is no life apart from the creator himself. For Montaigne, the new 'inner life' made it possible to replace blind obedience with reason which, precisely because it could not communicate with God, was free to turn itself upon the world. The reason of Montaigne was still very much the wisdom of the ancients, but Descartes was to transform it into something quite different. The seventeenth century was that of 'scientific theology'. For Pascal, however, man cannot do without the immediate presence of God.[1] The infinity of space is a thought that does not exalt, it frightens. Properly speaking, the 'Age of Faith' is that of the reformation, because then faith had to subsist without the aid of reason and in the long run it did not do very well. The fear and trembling, the ecstasy and terror which among the protestants could and did sometimes lead to insanity was the result of a maddening uncertainty, due less to the presence of God within oneself, than to his absence. There is no 'inner voice' that, during moments of terrible lucidity, we are not aware of having placed there ourselves, and the only way to be one of the Elect was to pretend to be one of them. Hence the hypocrisy which made of protestantism so peculiarly obnoxious a religion. The messiah, having failed to find God inside, needs to establish Him outside; he is therefore a partisan. The first great example of modern French prose, Pascal's *Lettres Provinciales*, is a pamphlet against the jesuits. Milton's pamphlets date from much the same time. On the other hand, Montaigne during the wars of religion was on the side of moderation and compromise: while the civil war might never have taken place for all we learn of it in Sir Thomas Browne. Montaigne's study was the first ivory tower, announcing the pre-eminence of mind. The 'Que sais-je?' was premature, for the Cartesian stove was the next

[1] It is this protestant exigence of immediacy in one's commerce with God which makes of Kierkegaard one of the fathers of existentialism. Reality, for the existentialist, is something of which we are conscious, not something we think.

18

ivory tower, independent even of books, one of the starting points from which reason set out on its incredible adventure. The monk is a peaceful man (Descartes like Montaigne and Sir Thomas Browne) whom we shall almost always find on the side of existing authority. Their God, neither terrible nor jealous, is that of fideism, inviting men to spiritual tranquillity, while the God of predestination is associated with spiritual torment; for God was less accessible in Himself, as an 'inner voice', than as the mind behind the creation.

However, knowledge considered as an immediate consciousness of the object rather than as an intellection of it was about to disappear, and the messiah will become more and more a man who derives an ethic from what others will be content to contemplate as an all-embracing Order; where others see a manifestation, he hears a summons. The seventeenth and eighteenth centuries mark a transition from religion as theology to religion as morality. So accustomed are we to associating religion and conduct, we forget that religion is primarily a means of making sense of the universe; it is a 'perception' before it is an ethic, and this is what one should bear in mind when reading the history of the papal courts. Catholicism still functions as an 'explanation', and is capable of an astonishing indulgence for those forms of political depravity which do not prejudice its interests. Protestantism reduces religion to little more than morality because the other dimensions of religious thought became the property of science. The only way to save God without falling into the intellectual petrification of the catholics was to bring him into one's life in the form of an unflaggingly virtuous conduct. It was by exemplary conduct that the protestant arrived at a kind of intimacy with God; he aimed at a level of moral accomplishment once required only of the priesthood and he therefore needed the priest's advantage of constant divine assistance.

The eighteenth century was not only the age of reason, it was the age of reason applied to conduct, an age in which the messianic and the contemplative were more or less united in the *philosophe*. It is at this time that objectivity in the modern sense began to emerge, for eighteenth-century thinking made the universality of scientific truth the criterion of all truth. Eighteenth-century optimism was founded upon the belief that the suppression of prejudice and superstition would bring about universal agreement on important issues including the political. Thus the *philosophe* combated religion as a fanaticism by advocating a tolerance which we now call objectivity.

19

Objectivity is faith in the possibility of universal agreement. But men can only be in agreement about objects which are identical for all of them; which is to say that objective thinking, including that of today, presupposes the existence of Absolutes just as does the thinking of the political fanatics. The difference between the monk and the messiah, as we have already remarked, is one not of essence but of method, the former being interested above all in intelligibility, the latter in giving intelligibility the form of an ethic. The history of socialism offers an excellent example of the conflict of these two types of mentality—the one being content to wait for the 'historical process' to overthrow capitalism, the other insisting that active co-operation would be indispensable. But in the idyllic eighteenth century, neither religion nor politics encouraged the choice men seem inevitably inclined to make—adore or obey. Contemplation and action were fused into one because Truth did not need to be established, but simply unveiled. The eighteenth century was the golden age of the intellectual, since in order to act one had only to combat ignorance. Word was deed because writing sought no more than to bring about official recognition of a *fait accompli*—the economic, cultural and political leadership of the bourgeoisie which had been slowly strengthening itself since the rebirth of cities in the middle ages. The war against religious fanaticism the rationalists won for humanity, their other campaigns they conducted for themselves, probably in good faith for the most part, since the labouring poor no more existed for them than they had at one time existed for the feudal lord. But after 1789, truth became a question of social class as it had once been a question of religious sect; once again it had to be established rather than simply revealed. The *philosophe* could suppose government amenable to universal agreement because the bourgeoisie was for a brief period alone in the field, monarchical divine right having been discredited, with that of the proletariat still to come.

There are those who love the gods and those who fear them. The protestant fear of God was in good part the fear of being abandoned by God, whose sympathy and interest was retained by an ethic of uncompromising austerity. If we may take Boswell to be a fairly representative young man of his time, then despite the Dr. Johnsons, it had clearly become difficult in the eighteenth century to keep religious precepts in the forefront of one's mind, and with the French revolution we pass from the age of religious to that of political

20

morality. In the meantime the tranquil faith of those who loved the gods was transforming itself into a faith in natural law; God had become little more than a word—deism. It was well that he should be there, but he no longer performed a vital task as he had in the universe of Descartes, and Berkeley was fighting a rearguard action. God had ceased altogether to intervene, and man should do the same. The world was admirably organized and would function perfectly if let alone. Men were wicked because society had corrupted a primitive goodness; commerce and industry went awry because governments interfered. It is disguised special pleading to maintain (as unfortunately many an academic is prepared to do) that learning need serve no practical purpose, and if such an argument is at all possible it is because scientific rationalism gave birth to another great myth of objective thought closely allied to that of universality, namely—the enunciation of a fact is equivalent to its utilization. If natural law is to perform its wonders, it must be free of human intervention. In this dispensation, contemplation is an act.

Dostoievski calls the revolutionaries of his time idolaters and not infidels. This is true of Voltaire, and it will be true of 'monastic' as well as of messianic thought throughout the nineteenth century. We have only to consider the tone with which Voltaire speaks not only of Newton but of anyone responsible for a scientific discovery to realize that worship had not ceased, it had shifted to another deity, the God of sweetness and light whose secrets were one by one being disclosed. The great systems of seventeenth-century scientific philosophy had been replaced by a more experimental science which proceeded by slow but inevitable and definitive accumulation. Voltaire catalogued and denounced the evils of his time, but for that very reason he could not, without a loathsome callousness, advise his readers to 'cultivate their gardens' unless he felt that these abuses were somehow 'accidents'. It is to be remarked that what Voltaire dwells upon in *Candide* for example, are, in general, evils which were to be mitigated with time (like those due to religious intolerance, the conduct of war, etc.) and not the evil which was, so to speak, 'built into the system'. In his *Siècle de Louis XIV*, he could write imperturbably: '. . . the labourer must have no more than the necessities of life if he is to work: such is the nature of man. The greater number must be poor, but not desperately so.' Had Voltaire been a planter he would have treated his slaves well, but he would not have been an abolitionist. Despite his deep and watchful passion

21

for justice, he was at peace with his times because the superstition and fanaticism he had fought against all his life were visibly yielding.[1] There was every reason to suppose that they would soon disappear altogether, and no reason to fear that they would shortly after be reborn with other names. Voltaire, that placid admirer of Louis XIV, had more of the monk than of the messiah. He was one of the new faithful, and if his faith is compatible with the belief that men will never find a way to abolish war, it is because the monk is satisfied with intelligibility, there will always be wars because 'such is the nature of man'. It is enough to know that the universe functions like clock-work. Intelligibility, however, is not enough for the messiah. He seeks to draw closer to the source of light through a propitiatory behaviour. To his class belong the guilt-ridden, the maladjusted, the restless, the sensitive, the intuitive—the Rousseaus of the earth.

We cannot continue without a few remarks about the irrationality with which romanticism (taken in its broadest sense) is often considered to have vitiated western thought. According to this view we are to count among the reasoners, the *ideologues*, the marxists, positivists, realists, empiricists, etc., and among the fomenters of unreason, romantics, some idealists, mystics, 'intuitionists' like Bergson, fascists, etc. What is meant here by 'irrationality'? Not a tendency to faulty reasoning, since the 'irrationalist' does not look upon reason as indispensable to the acquisition of the 'highest' knowledge. It is a question of the nature of the Absolute and consequently of the best means of communicating with it. The irrationalist was one who attempted to 'actualize' or make more concrete (whether through the 'divine afflatus' of the poet, some sort of intuition, or the many types of lay mysticism) an Absolute which the scientists and pseudo-scientists were content to assume. The romantics were fond of arguing that their incurable longing would be inexplicable unless man had known some sacred and splendid previous life to which he yearned to return. Romanticism is the thirst for an impossible reunion which we have already encountered in the protestant; except that, bereft of God, romanticism made a divinity of nature; or, more accurately, it made of nature a symbol or the outward expression of a divinity.

What strikes us most in retrospect when we think of the nineteenth

---

[1] The one exception to the Enlightenment's intellectual placidity is *Le Neveu de Rameau*. But this work is unique in the thinking of Diderot as well as in that of the eighteenth century as a whole.

century is its intense religiosity. Political thought was often an attempt to secularize paradise—to make a goal of what for the romantics had been an origin. The free-thinkers had their church in the masonic lodges; Nietzsche's revolt against God was at the same time an almost obsessive preoccupation with Him; Comte, the father of positivism, also fathered the 'religion of humanity'. It is a century of brutal antitheses—romanticism and realism, royalism and democracy, idealism and empiricism, not to mention the many derivatives of these terms. There was little place for nuance or bi-partisanship; men believed in final solutions to human problems either by denying their reality or by the invention of systems which resolved them. The rationalists were right to be impatient with romantic other-worldliness when it spread beyond poetry and one delights in the reference of Stendhal (who did not however make common cause with the rationalists) to M. Chateaubriand who 'defends religion as being pretty'.[1] And yet the anti-clericals could be as unreasoning as their adversaries. Flaubert's Homais had a faith as naïve and as uncritical as was that of the medieval peasant, and there was much of Homais in some of the nineteenth century's most eminent thinkers. Scientism had all of Voltaire's philosophic amateurishness along with a kind of fanaticism which was a result of the rapidly increasing control over nature that science was placing in men's hands. Scientism was a philosophy which confused *measured* reality with reality as a whole; it was that peculiar religion which worshipped the work of God, but not God himself; for we have now sufficiently recovered from the intoxication of science to see that most of nineteenth-century thinking is based upon the absurd postulation of a thought without a mind to think it. This was an absurdity that the seventeenth century had avoided, for it rightly felt that if the universe were to become a piece of machinery *that man could understand*, then philosophically God was more and not less necessary than ever before. Nineteenth-century rationalism was that of the eighteenth century with a much heightened consciousness of time, or evolution, and it often tried to outflank the difficulty I have mentioned by imagining the eventual deification of man himself.[2] Finalism, however, has a

[1] At least Chateaubriand did not attempt to defend religion on intellectual grounds—that was left for the twentieth century; perhaps because the communist is more feared than was the *sans-culotte*?

[2] André Gide was perhaps the last great representative of thinking of this kind.

way of trailing off into the religiosity which during the last century was as characteristic of the monk as of the messiah.

When one has assumed the existence of eternal and unalterable principles, whether one calls them scientific laws or God, there has been introduced an element of irrationality that no amount of reasoning will eliminate. Natural law, considered as equivalent to an 'understanding' of the universe, is not a discovery; it is man-made to satisfy man's need to know; and consequently, as Emile Meyerson remarks, science is metaphysical in its entirety for the simple reason that metaphysics is present at its inception. To be sure if one must believe in entities independent of space and time, then it is better to regard them as being germane to mind than to affectivity. But there is an obscurantism more exasperating even than the refusal to think, because it goes so well with a healthy appearance of lucidity—it is that of irrelevance, which is sometimes compatible with the keenest intelligence. We find this occasionally in Voltaire (as when he writes about Pascal), in writers like Anatole France, Bernard Shaw and Bertrand Russell, and in Julien Benda it becomes caricatural (*La France Byzantine*). The sweet reason of orthodox rationalism is like a water-wheel turning smoothly and effortlessly because it has been detached from its grindstone. The idyllic murmur of the great wheel of Anglo-Saxon empiricism is lulling an entire society to sleep. Great 'irrationalists' like Nietzsche and Péguy manage to be right again and again while their saner critics reason their way into insignificance or into some dangerously happy illusion. The work of Toynbee reminds us that there is no necessary connection between erudition and rationality; but if we ask Toynbee's more 'objective' detractors for their credentials, it will appear that they are the descendants of the nineteenth-century's laboratory technicians of history without the faith and hope. Toynbee wears his religiosity on his sleeve, his critics have repudiated theirs, but the wheel continues to turn as though nothing had happened. The objective scholar no longer believes in definitive answers, but he still conducts himself as though he were somehow performing a sacred function by adding another fact to the great store. Even when the purposelessness of this accumulation is honestly avowed, it is explained that inutility is an essential ingredient of true culture. This view results in there being more in the debris of Toynbee's historical thought than in a decade of the historical learned journals, just as there is more in the debris of Hegel (and what student of philosophy is not taught to snigger at

Hegel's mumbo jumbo?) than in all of British empiricism since Hume.

From these remarks it emerges that we cannot divide nineteenth-century thought (or, for that matter, all of Western thought) into the rational and the irrational, inasmuch as the reason of the rationalists is exercised in the name of an Absolute which is like the thought of a God divorced from the person of a God and which is as much the projection of a psychological need as is religious faith.

Such a re-appraisal cannot leave unaffected the terms objective and subjective as traditionally understood. The criterion of rational knowledge is its universality; it transcends the individual, it is independent of him, like an object; it is objective. And yet irrationality which is not mere insanity strives above all to quit the self, to be reunited with some 'higher' being or principle, whether disembodied spirits or nationality embodied in a dictator. The great examples of historical irrationality are not strictly speaking subjective, they are concerned with types of experience that the rationalist is either unequipped or poorly equipped to deal with, and which he therefore regards as 'subjective'; that is, as irrelevant to the pursuit of scientific truth. The 'irrationalist', the messiah, gives a face and a name to the divinity which the monk is satisfied to take for granted. 'Subjectivism' is simply an attempt to cope with problems which the rationalist brushes aside as meaningless or temporary.

Unfortunately, among these problems is that of existence itself. We saw that science in the beginning was 'platonic'; and even when it became more experimental it did not for that cease to be interested exclusively in 'essences' distilled from particulars. The sulphur used in laboratories is not much closer to sulphur in its natural state than is the ideal projectile of the law of inertia to a billiard ball. Add to this science's mistrust of sensory perception along with the disappearance of the notion of substance in contemporary physics, and we begin to appreciate that science and everyday life (which is commerce not only with the particular but with the unique) are at opposite poles. The argument, of course, had always been that science would eventually return to deal with particulars, assumed to be meaningless apart from some organizational principle. And this it has done with sensational success in what concerns the utilization of matter, but with none at all when it comes to a final understanding of matter, and with even less when it deals with the most important of all—not with man's relations with things, but his relations with

25

himself and with other men. Science is not a discovery but a choice.[1] At a given moment in history men choose to regard measurement as the fundamental reality; we have since come to see that measurement is but one aspect of reality, one that permits us to do much more with matter, but not one that is any nearer the 'Truth' than is, for example, the aristotelian qualitative view of the universe. In brief, it is existence (or choice) which is primordial, not science. Science is a tool, not a table of laws; hence the absurdity of looking to it for help in our decisions as to what a human life should be. And yet this absurdity is rooted in the objective thought of the monk. That science can offer no guide to, but must be guided by, the human, is an idea which in the course of the past half a century has had time to become a commonplace—it has apparently not had time to alter the outlook of that pseudo-scientist, the objective scholar. There is a conservatism of learning more tenacious than that of wealth because often the whole man is at stake, and not simply what he owns. Except in ages of faith (such as the nineteenth century) first principles will not bear close scrutiny, and if we examine those of the monk they will be seen to constitute a vicious circle.[2] Let me explain.

In science, the reward of objectivity is knowledge which sooner or later will compel universal consent. The eighteenth century believed that not only knowledge of things, but all knowledge might be of this kind; that is to say, it made an ethic of the objective observation of the exterior world. The apparently limitless potentialities of science as a means of subjecting nature to human control caused nineteenth-century thinkers to overlook the fact that there can be no natural law regulating human activities; for the discovery of such a 'law' would immediately present us with the choice of ignoring it or adhering to it, which would be incompatible with the idea of natural law as

[1] Even if one cannot accept Eddington's a priorism, he is still right in the sense that physics is concerned with aspects of reality so radically selective in nature and so far removed from ordinary perception that we can speak of creation as readily as of discovery; unless, of course, one still holds the view that science is progressing toward some final Truth which will somehow be more than another *scientific* truth.

[2] I should not perhaps be talking of principles here at all, for those in question have been so long outmoded that they have become simple prejudices. The intellectual's morality of objectivity like other moralities is something he lives by, or more exactly imagines himself to live by, something it does not occur to him to question. But while no one expects a religious morality to be coherent, one can presumably without unfairness ask the empiricist to justify his creed apart from faith.

generally understood. If man is ruled by laws not of his own making then necessarily he can never know them.[1] But even if we must abandon the concept of law to the physicist, the monk, it will be answered, still has in common with the scientist a laudable determination to be satisfied only with properly accredited facts and to withhold judgement in their absence. But whereas in science the establishment of a fact is usually accompanied by some practical utilization, the historian, sociologist, philosopher, etc., *cannot utilize his facts without ceasing to be objective.* Such is the vicious circle, which did not exist in the eighteenth century but which now emprisons the intellectual. If he remains objective he can accomplish nothing, if he tries to act he sacrifices his 'integrity'. There is an easy way out of the dilemma, however, which the monk has seized upon —he simply declares those facts most susceptible of troubling his peace of mind (his objectivity) to be outside his field of enquiry. Contemporary British philosophy offers a remarkable example of this procedure. Between the wars it announced that neither metaphysics nor ethics could form part of philosophy correctly understood. Insulated in this way against the burning problems of the day, whether they concerned the nation or the individual, the philosopher is able to reconcile objectivity with practical accomplishment. At the moment language is being found to offer a degree of innocuousness suitable for philosophical investigation. Basically, of course, this device is a genial extension of the principle of specialization. It is unnecessary here to go into the scandals of specialization in non-scientific disciplines; suffice it to say that surely never before has such a quantity of thinkers as are to be found in our universities offered so little to so many.

The messiah, therefore, is one who proposes to guide the common man whom the monk has abandoned out of consideration for objectivity. The great debate is not between the irrationalists and the rationalists, but between those who, in however vicious or misguided a fashion, try to face up to the problems of the day and those

[1] In the case of the individual, a neurosis is in a very real sense chosen by its victim who is therefore in some degree conscious of it; otherwise when the psychiatrist explains its nature and meaning the patient would not be able to recognize it as his own. Furthermore, to track down a neurosis successfully is not to exorcise a demon; for the patient then has to choose whether with the help of a clearer understanding, he is going to combat his obsessions or continue to yield to them. There is a third possibility, that of a cure effected, so to speak, against one's will; but such 'cures' are but slightly more attractive than the disease itself.

who refuse to do so. The monk who is not simply a cynic must, however obscurely, subscribe to the christian dogma of the eventual triumph of the Good; for he can surely have no illusions as to how often fact, reduced to itself, is able to prevail over fiction. The conception of truth as self-imposing, which the monk must acknowledge as his if he is not to be inexcusable, is more irrational than the messiah's efforts toward a closer communication with the Absolute by substituting action for contemplation. This in addition to the fact that the scholar is as much a metaphysician as is the revolutionary, the difference being that the revolutionary identifies his Absolute and is therefore often obliged to twist the facts to suit it, while the scholar continues prudently to deal with an Absolute for the moment conjectural, whose function will eventually be to synthesize the facts into one glorious whole. The revolutionary is therefore 'subjective' in the sense that he sometimes sees facts more as he wishes them than as they really are. But the marxist revolutionary is considered to stem from the rationalist, or objective tradition, and the answer here is not that over-zealous rationalists may deviate into subjectivism, but that, like the mystics, they may push objectivity to such an extreme that the Object becomes real enough to enable them to sacrifice everything else in its name.

If the objective intellectual fails to recognize himself in the portrait I have drawn of him, it is because he has come to consider the universe as being meaningless in the sense that it contains no absolute truth accessible to mind. But if this is one's point of view, then it must be recognized that our traditional schools of thought are not to be divided into the rational or the irrational, since by their faith in final answers they are both irrational. The difference is rather one of *temperament*, and there are, broadly speaking, two types which I have called the monastic and the messianic.

Temperament lies deeper than thought, and it is in vain that the intellectual should have come to think differently, for instead of seeing in the new-found meaninglessness of the universe a now unobstructed field for the exercise of human enterprise, he discovers the inutility of effort. It is in this way that he keeps abreast of the times while continuing to enjoy the contemplative passivity which characterizes the monk. But if effort in an absurd world is pointless it is because it can achieve nothing *definitive*, and we see that the monk remains at heart the absolutist I accuse him of being.

The messiah is everywhere in discredit; no one has a kind word
28

for the system-builder; he is responsible for all our ills. There is no harm in accepting this, and from now on less will be said about the messiah. But what are we to think of the objective intellectual who, from the bankruptcy of systematic thought as it has existed in the past, appears to have concluded the bankruptcy of thought in general? What are we to do with the thinker who no longer considers it his business to think?

Determinism is an aspect of reality much insisted upon by classical physics, and there was ample justification for extending the notion from things to men, for one does not define a man, he is whatever he takes himself to be. He is self-creative. He is 'caused' by this or that if he so wishes. There is much impotent longing in romanticism. The marxist might point out that most of the romantics were aristocrats and that their longing was therefore caused by their loss of power and prestige as a class; they looked to the past because it had been theirs. The freudian might explain that the romantic state of mind is caused by an unconscious memory of the comforts of the womb. The economists, the anthropologists, and the others could, with a little effort, find causes better to their liking. All these views are right in that they note aspects of a given reality; they are all wrong in that it is no longer considered useful to dwell upon the causal aspects of reality, and soon cause in the old sense will have ceased to interest us. Our perception will have changed.

It is impossible for us to see an object in its entirety with a single glance. The 'points of view' we necessarily occupy in respect to it are limitless in number, and each of them presents, perceptually, a different object, which is yet always the same. This cannot be altogether true of the universe we live in because that is an object of which we are a part. We are not 'at a distance' from it; it is therefore an object we cannot identify once and for all because we can compare it to no other. At the same time, although we may adopt many points of view, only one is completely 'in focus'; it is that brought before us by the slow displacement of history. The perspective offered by historical circumstance involves truths which are in a sense absolute—because the universe is 'unknowable', there is no exhaustive truth and we cannot, except in imagination, transcend the epoch in which we are born, we cannot change our perception. And yet these truths are not absolute because there have been many others in the past, and there are many others to come. The world as we see it both is and is not the 'real' world. Our truths are the only truths and yet there are others.

If we accept this view, and the only obstacle is the belief that science is the Truth and not simply an aspect of the truth, an unwillingness to see that while scientific truth will always be 'true', it will, indeed for the sake of all of us it *must*, come to be regarded as irrelevant to whatever touches upon man himself who is choice and not thing—if then we accept this view we shall be led to a number of important conclusions of concern to the objective intellectual.

If only for the sake of 'objectivity', no quality would seem more indispensable to the intellectual than a mentality of seismographic delicacy prepared to register the slightest tremors in the world of thought. And yet the series of tremendous shocks which on the continent have destroyed most of the time-worn perspectives of occidental thought have not been recorded by British instruments. The public has been informed that, in reality, nothing took place, that the continentals, and particularly the French with their customary levity, have simply invented a number of new philosophical terms which mean nothing but which may be so combined as to appeal to the emotions of the unwary.[1]

Changes are nevertheless occurring which may be as far-reaching as those which transformed the middle ages into the renaissance; and from new vantage points we discover that the disputes of the past all took place within a framework of principles and attitudes which betray a common spiritual need or orientation, of which we must try to free ourselves. If the world has a meaning (and until very recently no one ever seriously doubted that it did) then, since life for anyone but a fool is more often than not a sorry affair, it is a meaning that is *hidden*. This is the beginning of philosophy, and science simply carries on the age-long hunt by somewhat different means. Bacon spoke of the *latens schematismus*, or hidden form of objects. Behind appearance there is a Reality, which is intelligible and which is one. Although, unlike some of the Greek philosophers and the christian theologians, scientists and scientific philosophers have been hesitant about naming the One, they have bequeathed a host of lesser hidden 'realities' whose names we use without realizing

[1] The insularity of British philosophy is not absolute since linguistic philosophy may be considered a faint echo of phenomenology in that the former takes the same view of language as the latter takes of things; that is, the meaning of a word is its use just as the appearance of a thing is its reality. But the discovery that a statement means what it says, hardly seems worth dwelling upon.

that we are dealing with pure suppositions. No one, for example, knows what 'mind' is, or whether any such entity exists, but that did not prevent philosophers from going ahead with exhaustive analyses of what it 'contains' and how it functions. No one has ever seen a species or a natural law (but in the case of law, it is true, Hume issued a warning that did not go altogether unheeded). Who knows what 'normality' is? Perhaps it is what 'nature intended' and is to be found in the 'average man'. It is easy to forget that one's 'unconscious' is a word and not a thing. The study of literature and art is often little more than a search for the hidden 'influences' which certainly exist but whose precise effect and importance no one could in most cases calculate even if there were any profit or interest to be derived from such a calculation. Historians conduct themselves as though the past were a great warehouse in which a number of precious items (no one knows exactly what) have unfortunately been misplaced. In reality, nothing has been lost, for the past is determined by the present. The first world war, for example, was not one of the 'causes' of fascism between the wars; in their terror of communism, the democracies allowed fascism to grow strong, and historians discovered or rediscovered the general rule that wars breed totalitarianism. History, of course, confirmed the rule, as it will confirm any rule which is not too fanciful.

There is no great historical thought apart from a determination to use the past in the shaping of the future. This is the greatness of Marx and the smallness of his critics. It is interesting to remark here that the objective historian uses the same device we admired a moment ago in the hands of the philosopher—he defines history in such a way as to make it amenable to his talents; thus Marx is not a historian, just as the moralist or metaphysician is not a philosopher. The most disastrous effect of scientism has been to produce a kind of mentality for which determinism is not a doctrine but an ingrained intellectual habit of which the victim very often is not even aware. Who can fail to be struck by the extent to which the intellectual's thinking is historical, as though the past were a decision irrevocably handed down like the judgement upon Adam and Eve, our business being to interpret the judgement upon which depends the future. To be sure, historians no longer think in this way, but that is what I mean by asserting that determinism, having ceased to be a doctrine, persists as a habit. For if historians are not looking for 'secrets' in the past which are to determine the future (and let us bear in mind

31

that those secrets are not precious for helping us to mould the future, because that involves 'taking sides', it involves the sacrifice of one's objectivity, which could result in writings like the *Communist Manifesto* rather than articles of permanent interest for the learned journals), then how are they to justify their position in our society which is that of a man seated on the rear of a lorry examining the road behind while an incompetent driver moves on at a reckless speed in what is possibly the wrong direction?

Our learning is therefore the domain of the hidden or the nonexistent. It seems that what *is* can only be explained by what we can neither see, hear nor touch—atoms, the unconscious, the past, and so forth. The scientist as well as the intellectual is one who 'oversimplifies' the real, which could not otherwise be expressed. It is over-simplified in the sense that it is considered to be 'visible' (i.e. comprehensible) in its entirety or in large part from a single point of view, which is necessarily inaccessible to the senses capable of seizing the real only in a perspective blurred by the subjectivity of time and place. This nonexistent point of view from which all is visible is that of objectivity, which is, therefore, in the final analysis, a foredoomed attempt to transcend time and place. When God was chased from his earthly paradise of the middle ages, he became an objective thought; for only God is timeless and omnipresent. But objectivity, despite its concealed religiosity, was once a noble conquest. It is now a pallid religion indeed, with a very easy morality.

There is much of Greek philosophy in christian theology; there is an identity of first principles to which we are probably indebted for the preservation of Greek culture. Our thought has never ceased to be readily adaptable to the needs of the messiah, it has never ceased to be concerned almost exclusively with the everlasting and the immutable; it has remained 'essentialist'. The intellectual is an essentialist by his passion for definition which he takes to be a wholesome thirst for clarity. What is art? What is man, woman, the novel, democracy, etc.? They are, of course, what we make of them; but the intellectual plays too small a role in the making of anything for such an idea to be agreeable to him. A definition permits him to pass from the immediate where things are done or made to the realm of the ageless where nothing ever happens. The historian (and every academic is a historian of something) is to be compared to the military theoretician. The only way to test a military theory in preparation for war is to consult the history of warfare. But this is almost invariably done at the expense of improvisation, and the result is a disaster. Genuine thought is thought about present experience, and the aged have ceased to think because they have ceased to experience. The academic is prematurely aged, his mind moves effortlessly through the husks of digested events.

Is it inevitable that we continue trying to explain what exists by what does not exist, the seen by the unseen, the present by the past? Must we go on living on faith—in God, in science, or in the countless mystifications of the intellectual—and continue to mistrust the evidence of our senses? Yes, if we insist upon explanations. But what if (as most of us already obscurely believe) there are no explanations, what if things go wrong not because there are some answers we are still waiting for, but because there are those among us who seek to make them go wrong? What, for example, if prices rise not because of this or that economic 'law' but (as we perfectly well know) because certain individuals find it in their interest to raise prices? Is it not time to admit that crime and vice are not 'aberrations' but choices more or less freely arrived at? If they were aberrations, they would not fascinate us; and there is as much humanity in the Marquis de Sade as in a century of English literature.[1] Wars are not 'explained' like earthquakes by the events which precede them; they are willed by certain men with the help of the objectivity of the world's academic communities or of the intelligentsia in general, whose silence (the messianic reaction being, for reasons we have discussed, invalid) is naturally interpreted by the people as assent or indifference. Evil, in brief, is not an accident of the substance good; it is built into the scheme of things for the simple reason that men are free to choose it. Only in its petty forms is it sometimes dependent upon ignorance; when it occurs massively, as in fascism, it is never the fruit of ignorance. The concept of objectivity is tenable only if one supposes evil to be a negative quality fated to disappear with the progress of enlightenment. We have come far from this view, and yet it is still much with us in the form of a belief —so deep-rooted that it often escapes detection—that the True and the Good are somehow of the same stuff, as aesthetes like to believe

[1] Anyone with experience of middle-class respectability (to which sections of the working class seem to be acceding) understands how a man can choose to be a safe-breaker, and may admire him for his choice. The underworld is becoming the last refuge of independence of mind and conduct.

in the oneness of the True and the Beautiful. Or, if evil is never to disappear, is not the objective attitude (one not blinded by the suffering which makes a partisan) the point from which evil may be seen to be an essential part of the whole; that is, not evil at all? *Tout comprendre, c'est tout pardonner.*

Suppose we abandon the superstition of the objective point of view from which all is visible—the hidden vantage point of God. Why not give up the myth of the cave (a reassessment every two thousand years does not appear excessive) and turn our attention from what we do not know and perhaps can never know, to what we do know. Habits of thought can be, and are being, entirely reorganized upon this basis. Our freedom as human beings, if not always as individuals, runs deeper than the freedom of act; it is constitutive of the world about us. The importance of art is that the 'vision' of a great artist, if it becomes that of an important artistic movement, will also, eventually, become that of all men. Modern architecture, not to mention the design of countless industrial products, would have been unthinkable without the reviled and still misunderstood cubists. Perception, however, is not constitutive of the world in the Kantian sense. For post-renaissance philosophy there is only one world, the 'true' world, that of science; while we are postulating a multitude of worlds, which are yet the same. Since we are a part of the world, it is meaningless to seek its 'real' nature, and consequently that view of things which is ours, thanks to a given historical situation, is not an appearance behind which the Truth lies hidden, the *appearance is reality.* There is no 'objective' world which Cézanne and his followers perversely flouted. The world of Cézanne is that of Delacroix, and yet it is altogether different—just as the great philosopher thinks new ideas which he has nevertheless inherited. The world is not a substance which we mould to suit our fancy or which the categories of the mind render intelligible, but rather an object of infinite complexity toward which we may adopt various points of view which will be not more or less 'true' but more or less rewarding in terms of human well-being. I cannot agree with Malraux that 'non-representational' art is a 'second creation' quite independent of the first. The vision of the artist is anchored in the real, but the real is not the same for every culture. The wish to 'copy nature' appears to me always to have been fundamental in art; all art is representational. What changes is the opinion as to what constitutes nature; or, at least, the proper vantage point from which to represent it.

We now view nature as 'absurd', not in the sense of meaningless, but in the sense that it can never be fully expressed in a form which we shall not sooner or later find to be inadequate, and it is this nature that cubism 'copies'. Little importance is to be attached to technical proficiency in art, and there is perhaps no cause to wonder at the admirable drawings that men living some fifty thousand years ago left on the walls of their caves. The sculptors of Moissac were not less competent than those of fifth-century Greece; the difference was that they did not see the human body as did the Greeks; they were copying a nature that was totally different.

If, then, orthodox western art is not so much the product of a tradition which has acquired, more thoroughly than any other, the means of representing nature as it 'really is'; if, rather, it is the expression of a world view that can be and is being supplanted, then how are we to characterize this view now that we have in modern art a standard of comparison which is not that of another culture or of another age?

For the messiah, Order is a dispensation of God and not God a dispensation of Order; and morality, therefore, is still a matter of primordial importance. But the position of the messiah was always a difficult, often an 'irrational' one; the protestants fervently solicited a God who had yet 'predestined' them, and later revolutionaries sought to take a hand in the functioning of an inevitable historical process. The messiah's mistrust or even hatred of art which is not didactic with a painful literalness springs from the outrage which a soul oppressed by a sense of moral urgency feels upon contact with the amoral supra-human timelessness characteristic of the best representational art. Tolstoi's attempt at a complete revaluation of western art is typical of the messiah's reaction to an art which, with the possible exception of the Greek, was the first to aim quite consciously at the production of beautiful objects, objects divorced from immediate sacred utility and whose chief value resides in the expression of a nameless, and in this sense a *hidden*, eternal Order which we may contemplate but not approach. This is the art of the monk which, despite the advent of cubism (not to mention the transformation of poetry and music which help to confirm the impression that a fundamental change is taking place), many of us persist in regarding as 'true' art.

We need not insist upon the notion of order as far as form is concerned. Nothing is clearer than the 'mathematization' of post-

35

medieval art—perspective in painting, increasingly rigid form in poetry, symmetry in architecture, etc. But how is this art expressive of that order which men had begun to see everywhere and which was thrusting the sacred beyond the reach of physical perception? The middle ages shade imperceptibly into the renaissance—there is nothing like the abruptness with which modern art surges upon the scene—and that evolution is to be regarded not as the gradual emergence of the individual from feudal anonymity, but rather as the transformation of the individual into the type, and this is accomplished by the suppression of detail; or, if one prefers, by the separation of the individual from his environment. In passing from the microscopic detail of the illuminated manuscript, or the complexity of a Gothic façade to the lunar backgrounds of Leonardo, the non-finito of Michelangelo, or the plain surfaces of Brunelleschi, we pass from the concrete to the abstract, from the present to the eternal, from existence to essence. There can be no greater error than to suppose medieval art oriented in the direction of the hereafter and renaissance art toward the here and now. The reverse is true because the other-worldly formed, as we have seen, a perceptual part of medieval life; the 'miraculous' was a daily occurrence, it was anecdotal. The artist, therefore, could be explicit to the full extent of his patience. No limit was set to the profusion of detail because 'one cannot know too much'; this art was intended to be instructive, not beautiful. Even the noble statues of Chartres are those of individuals, each bearing in his hands an object which identifies him; but Michelangelo's 'prisoners' are anonymous, his reclining figures in the Medici chapel are symbolic, the Medici themselves idealized, and has not little David become Goliath, while Moses is splendid enough to be God himself? In portrayals of the virgin, the landscape, the wise men, the stables, the animals, all gradually disappear, and the virgin ceases to be an individual named Mary to become a symbol of motherhood. Gothic art was interested only in the clothed figure because clothing serves to situate and to identify; the nude is an abstraction, an 'essence'. For pre-renaissance people, the world was a vast theatre where the extra-terrestial, as under the walls of Troy, haggled daily for men's souls. But as time went on, art ceased to be an eye-witness account of a victory or a defeat, and began to mirror the eternal. Even in the case of the portrait, the personage is depicted, not as his friends knew him, but *'tel qu'en lui-même l'éternité le change'*. He is shown in the full regalia of office, as his wife herself

36

rarely saw him, and the artist has striven to bring out the hidden nobility of countenance which naturally accompanies high station. Often, of course, the individual is simply a model, helping the painter to fix upon canvas the essence of an emotion or occupation. Pater could never have brought himself to look upon La Gioconda as a mere woman; whatever the intention of Leonardo, the portrait is made to be precious in the degree of its suggestiveness, in the degree to which it stimulates not the vision, but the mind. The virgin of medieval art does not lend herself readily to flights into the ideal, she is so much of the earth that she must wear a halo to prove that she is not just one of us.

What happens with the renaissance, therefore, is that the artist ceases to depict the sacred itself, since the sacred is no longer perceived, and begins to present it as seen in or through individuals or landscapes. The greatness of God had once been his ability to violate order whenever it pleased him, hence the frequence of 'miracles'; but with the coming of science God's greatness began to reside in that awe-inspiring omniscience which had created an Order so perfect that intervention was never necessary. Spinoza went so far as to assert that this Order *was* God himself. But whether God himself or only a reflection of him, it is clear that the function of the artist is to copy as faithfully as possible the world about him because it is all sacred if only we know how to look at it. The medieval artist was a teller of tales. He told of the irruption of the sacred into the more ordinary course of affairs, he recorded events. The modern pre-cubist artist will be, like the scientist, an investigator; for the sacred is not a happening, it is a substratum, it is hidden, and art must try to bring it out. If this were to be achieved, the content of art would have to be 'simplified'. The result was the distinction between landscape and portrait painting, and the separation of sculpture from architecture. The landscape or the individual could be taken separately because each in its own way mirrored the Divine Plan, while previously the individual could not be lifted from his surroundings since it was there that he lost or won salvation. We may regard the famous 'individualism' of the renaissance as simply the gradual elimination of the choruses of saints and angels, a gradual secularization. In brief, it is no longer the identity of the individual which renders art sacred, it is art which renders the individual sacred (though this tendency will not reach its limit until romanticism) by emphasizing the 'eternal' at the expense of the

37

transitory. The idea of art for art's sake, which was to kill the classical tradition in western art by making it clear that such art had nothing more to say, was therefore present at the beginning; but we must not allow art for art which has had an enormous influence upon our thinking about aesthetics blind us to the existence of the 'sacred' in post-renaissance art simply because with the renaissance it ceased to have a name, simply because the halo disappears. We do not know what Leonardo's John the Baptist is pointing at, but he is most certainly pointing, and Pater is closer to the truth than is Berenson.

The renaissance makes an attempt to reach God through the world rather than in spite of it. The artist becomes, very self-consciously in the case of poets, a bestower of immortality. But one does not immortalize individuals as such, they are first made to represent this or that aspect of cosmic order. Love sonnets are addressed to perfect women, and the patron prince is the long-awaited realization of an ideal. In renaissance tragedy, it was not only an individual who came to grief, but the image a society had of itself, the representative of a tiny oligarchy, at once a propitiatory offering and the proud declaration of a right to do battle with the gods. The tragic hero was not a type, types are figures of comedy, he was the objectification, the definition of an ethic; and tragedy dies when the definition is no longer taken for granted, when a society can no longer successfully portray its ideal in a single person; and when, therefore, the tragic conflict takes place between differing notions of man and not within the hero himself. The hero in tragedy is a person of terrible vulnerability because the opinion he has of himself is identical with that which others have of him. It is possible for the ordinary man to 'make peace with himself', but tragedy comes about precisely because subjective yearnings cannot be satisfied without the sacrifice of an objective identity in which the hero recognizes the greater part of his value as a man. This is not a mere question of reputation, for allegiance was owed to a Self which was part of the scheme of things—the divinity which hedged in kings was shared by every tragic hero. Unless one is a scholar engaged in the increasingly lonely, where not hypocritical, business of 'appreciating', it is difficult to enter into the spirit of the hero's concern for something for which we do not even have a word, and which is perhaps best designated by a term borrowed from the French classical theatre—*gloire*. We have made of Othello a vulgar romantic

38

driven half mad by jealousy. But the killing of Desdemona was not an act of passion; it was a calculated execution, almost, one might say, in the interests of state. There is a joy in revenge, however fleeting, which was denied Othello because the sacrifice of Desdemona was the fulfilment of a duty toward an objective self which knew nothing of love and which would hear only of honour, of *gloire*. There is no solution for the tragic hero because he is summoned to choose between two selves, neither one of which he can live without. This is tragic 'inevitability'. Lear is pure tragedy in the sense that the hero's possibility of action, that is, his hope, is reduced to a minimum because his honour is entirely in the keeping of his daughters. *Hamlet* is at the other extreme. The hero's *gloire* is so completely under his own protection that no one has satisfactorily explained why it was not at once vindicated and tragedy avoided. Othello is a nobler personage than is Macbeth because Othello fulfilled his obligations towards himself while Macbeth betrayed them. His was the tragedy of self-contempt. If Corneille is a lesser tragedian than Racine or Shakespeare, it is because his heroes are too heroic; the exigencies of the objective self are too certain to prevail over the longings of subjectivity. The 'moral law' has no place in tragedy. Racine's Phaedra sins not against the gods but against herself—the daughter of Minos and wife of Theseus. Every tragic hero is a kind of Prometheus, owing allegiance to himself (that is, to the divinity in man) and being persecuted by the gods, to whom we are as 'flies to wanton boys'; or, in the words of Phaedra:

> Ces dieux qui se sont fait une gloire cruelle
> De séduire le coeur d'une faible mortelle.

For there to be tragedy, there must be approximate equality between the demands of the 'mere man' and what the hero considers he owes himself. But also the objective self must embody a lofty ideal, or at least lofty responsibilities. There is consequently no bourgeois tragedy because ideals are here stained with self-interest or mediocrity; the 'divinity' has quite disappeared. On the other hand, there is neither a christian nor a communist tragedy because the 'divine' totally escapes individual control; in the confessions of the one and the auto-criticisms of the other, it is a matter of principle that the subjective be denounced and the public self, the tool of divine or historical law, vindicated.

Classical art, therefore, like classical science, abhors the subjective.

The classical conception of beauty involves looking beyond the individual represented to the objective generality which is 'conveyed', just as science looked beyond individuals to the 'law' which 'explained' them. If, as has often been remarked, science in its highest theoretical reaches begins to resemble art, it is true also that art is a tireless demonstration of the order and harmony which science tries to make explicit. The geometry of perspective and of proportion proposed to capture a reality independent of time and place, like that objective identity of the hero to which he tragically sacrificed or tragically failed to sacrifice his particular concupiscence.

If such is reality, then it is no longer what we see that counts, but what we think. This new 'perception' required a new faculty, which proceeded to assume a number of forms: the cogito, the conscience of the protestants, the reason of the eighteenth century, the ego of the idealists and the romantics, etc. The individualism which has come down to us from the renaissance through humanism has nothing to do with subjectivity; indeed it is quite the opposite, since it postulates the greatness of and the rights of the individual only in so far as he possesses a given mental apparatus functioning in a given way; it is not concerned with the individual in so far as he *differs* from other individuals. In brief, since it was unthinkable that the Real should not be the same for all men, and since the Real was what was thought, then men must have an essential characteristic in common—an intellect, that divine spark which had come to supplement the soul. The new-found greatness of man lay precisely in his possession of this channel of communication with the divine plan. Man had been taken into the Lord's confidence.

The error of the art for art aesthetic, which though discredited has not been replaced, is to suppose that because the great artist ennobles whatever he touches, he is indifferent as to what he touches. It is not style that makes a great writer, it is having something great to say, and it is the conviction with which it is said that gives birth to style. The painter has something to say in the sense that he is trying to get at reality. Our preoccupation with formal values should not therefore cause us to neglect the artist's 'message'—his conception of the Real. We shall never know what to make of modern art for as long as we persist in looking at it *sub species aeternita*, for as long as we try to bind it to the past to avoid fracturing our definitions. It marks nothing less than the advent of a new world view differing from that of classical art perhaps even more deeply than scientific perception

40

differs from that of medieval aristotelianism. To be sure, one would have no right to such a conviction were it based upon an examination of art alone. If the Real for Braque or Picasso is of a totally different nature from what it was for Constable, then we should expect, if Braque and Picasso are really to be placed among the greatest of painters (that is, if this new reality is to be taken seriously), that our conception of the mental undergo a change as it did at the end of the middle ages. This has indeed happened; but before coming to that we must try to decide what aspect of reality the cubists consider to be the proper concern of art; in other words, what they consider to be the truth about things.

One is tempted, with Malraux, to dismiss the whole question, to turn it over to the aesthetes and the art historians by affirming that cubism does not depict anything, it is pure creation; a cubist painting is not a picture of something, but an object in its own right. In this way, we keep to the solid ground of purely formal values, but at the same time we reduce the artist to a kind of decorator, or manufacturer of curios. Malraux cannot save him with talk of a 'second creation', for in the case of modern art, Malraux is compelled to argue that the 'second creation' is inspired by itself alone—our art is a monument to itself. But if this were true, we should be back to art for art in an aggravated form, for now we need not be content with simply minimizing the importance of content, we can suppress it altogether. No one can sensibly argue that the artist must 'serve the people', but it is even more inadmissible that he should fail to be deeply involved in the particular agonies and perplexities of his time, that he should fail to voice in unmistakable terms his own age. In unsettled times, great artists have a way of being on the 'right side', and while their partisanship may not be good for their art, it is not necessarily bad; thus Picasso's Guernica is a very great painting. Inversely, we should expect a Dali to reconcile himself with a corrupt régime because he is a charlatan. Men are all of a piece; if their thinking is rotten or non-existent, so is their art. Art for art is essentially a refusal to choose, the refusal being made in the name of art, just as, in the case of the monk, it is made in the name of objectivity. The result is poor art and poor thought. Flaubert is one of the greatest of the spokesmen for this general abstentionism whose facility alone should have rendered it suspect. In a letter to Louise Colet, he had this to say: 'In an age like ours, I even believe that a thinker (and what is the artist if not a triple thinker?) should have neither religion nor nationality nor even any political conviction. Absolute doubt appears to me so clearly demonstrated that to wish to express it would be almost a stupidity.' And further along he concludes: 'Let us do our duty, which is to write well.' Thinkers without thoughts except to write well were to proliferate in proportion as it became more and more vital for men to have political convictions. But unluckily one cannot both write well and be persuaded that there is nothing to say; and Flaubert is consequently a much lesser artist than Stendhal or Dostoievski, whose point of departure is conviction and not the lack of it.

In painting, of course, much more than in writing, the need for artistic independence must come close to being the fundamental conviction, and if I deplore the art for art aesthetic latent in Malraux's view, it is not because I believe that artists must have strong political convictions but because now, as in the fourteenth century with Giotto, art is saying something new, and we shall not understand what it is if we persist in supposing formal values to be the very substance of art. 'Vision' has taken precedence over technique, and the philosopher is better placed to understand the new perception than is the art historian.

Has art during the past fifty years or so really turned in upon itself and ceased to represent the world about us? We can do no better here than ask the artist himself what he is trying to accomplish. Let us therefore take Cézanne, from whom cubism stems, and Braque, who is still at work. One can easily read Cézanne's letters and overlook the one precept to which he returns most insistently, and which is very nearly his only one—'copy nature'. Here are two examples out of many I might have chosen. 'But I must always come back to this: painters must devote themselves entirely to the study of nature and try to produce pictures which are an instruction.' Or again: 'Now the theme to develop is that—whatever our temperament or power in the presence of nature may be—we must render the image of what we see, forgetting everything that existed before us.' But this seems an outrageous commonplace coming from a painter of Cézanne's stature: and then, he did not 'copy nature' anyway, one would think, since it is with him that the systematic 'distortion' begins that was to culminate in people like Braque. Nevertheless, in his conversations with Jean Paulhan, Braque, like Cézanne, strikes us as a man making use of his art to record the results of an infinitely painstaking and lifelong investigation of the

42

things around him. Braque used to carry his paintings with him into the country: '. . . to introduce them to things', he says, 'to see whether they [the paintings] would stand up to it.' Another remark: 'If I put a piece of white paper on this blotter, I see it before the blotter. I see it in relief. I worked on that.' If we take refuge in formal values in talking of the work of a Braque, it is to avoid the unclean contact of the 'subjective'. If Braque is copying nature, we say, then it is far too subjective a one to be worth our attention. But this is a mistake. Vision is a habit. We see only what we look for, what we consider we 'should see', what our education has taught us to see. We are taught to see a given aspect of reality just as we are taught to speak a given language; but there are other aspects, as there are other languages. People who work in noisy factories soon grow unconscious of the noise; but the noise is still there, just as is the world of Braque, whether or not we are conscious of it. The scientific view of the world has led us to believe in the existence of a *single* objective reality, with our perception being not a passive absorption, but an act of discrimination calculated to reveal to us the world as it 'really is'. We may therefore define 'scientific perception' as one in which the judgement intervenes to 'correct' what is seen. A painter called upon to reproduce the image of a straight stick thrust into water will show the stick as it *appears* to be—as bent; and yet the same painter will depict a landscape as it 'really is'. From my window I can see a stretch of lawn in the distance, it appears to be a green wall; I can also see a tower and the cloud appears to be pressing in upon it from all sides. Why should I not paint the lawn as a wall and the tower as jutting into some white fluffy solid? If the intellect is not allowed to interfere in the case of the stick, on what grounds is it allowed to do so in the case of the lawn? It will be said that if we go to the lawn we shall be able to walk across it and shall not have to climb over it; and climbing the tower will not enable us to touch the clouds. But the artist is required to paint what he sees, not what he knows. In *Etruscan Places*, Lawrence speaks of this subtle interference of knowledge with vision: 'For a man who sees, sees not as a camera does when it takes a snapshot, not even as a cinema camera taking its succession of instantaneous snaps; but in a curious rolling flood of vision, in which the image itself seethes and rolls; and only the mind *picks out* certain factors which *shall* represent the image seen.' Modern art is quite simply an attempt to present the image itself unprocessed by the mind. We may therefore assert unhesitatingly that, in copying nature, modern art is more rigorous than the classical. The 'otherworldliness' I spoke of as characteristic of traditional art arises from the fact that the artist paints not what he sees but an ideal, objective, and to some extent non-existent world that is the *same* no matter from what angle it is viewed. The artist 'corrects' what he sees so that the finished work is less a copy than a construction.

We may now go a step further to recall that no artist worthy of the name is content to deal with appearances, he copies reality. In science, the hidden is more real than the apparent which we must mistrust, and the same is true of the art that accompanied science in its rise to power. Reality, which was once hidden, is found in modern art on the surface of things which *are what they appear to be*. The classical artist begins to paint with an unconscious assumption of the greatest importance—that objects have a given, unchanging identity; an objective identity which we must know since we cannot rely upon its always being seen. The cubist refuses to consider such knowledge as relevant to the pursuit of his art—a bit of newspaper incorporated into his composition is no longer a bit of newspaper. The world of cubism is one in which objects exist in and for themselves, before the mind has given them objective identities; it is the palpable world of vision, not the hidden one of knowledge. This is what Braque expresses when he defines painting as being concerned with: 'objects put out of use' (*des objets désaffectés*).

For half a century or so, the tidy world of fixed identities (or uses) has been disintegrating to the advantage of what has come to be called the absurd. The absurd as a purely negative conception of a universe which, in the final analysis, does not make sense has enjoyed wide acceptance. It enables the poet to suffer in the midst of plenty and the monk to demonstrate the naïvety of engaging in constructive action. But we have just seen that the cubist copies reality, a reality in which objects are intelligible in themselves, in which they are independent of any principle of total organization. A reality furthermore that is objective (since the lawn appears as a wall to everybody) but which is at the same time subjective in that the objective mind imagined by classical philosophy no longer has a function.

We have seen in the introduction that subjectivity being a nothingness does not reason its way through appearance to reality. It must find intelligibility in every object; and yet, there being no Absolute thanks to which reality is definitely this or that, intelligibility must be the result of what subjectivity 'intends', of the way in which it orientates itself. Subjectivity both receives and constitutes meaning (we shall see exactly how this occurs when we come to consider the philosophy of Sartre): the cubist paints a world that has undergone no mental processing; and yet it is one he has constituted by discovering that objects are very different from what the classical artist supposed them to be.

It might be well now to restate in a few words the ideas that have so far been presented.

The intellectual is primarily a man engaged in trying to make sense of the world. If he succeeds, he may proceed to act; he becomes a messiah. Others, more cautious, are always sceptical of these 'successes'; they prefer to wait and to protect our cultural heritage by compiling facts about it—these are the monks. In recent years, some monks have come to believe that no sense is to be made of the world, and that its present wretched state is largely the work of the messiah who, in his blind certitude, is prepared to sacrifice means to ends. This usually involves a contempt for facts, and the monk has made it his business to protect them—he is objective. The absurd, however, is as destructive of objectivity as of system; but to understand why, we must be more clear as to what objectivity is.

Objectivity is a perception. It is the scientific perception which came into existence with the renaissance. People of the middle ages saw God and his Order; but the Order postulated by science is attained by mind, not vision; that is to say, it is objective, independent of time and place, as is, necessarily, the mind that thinks it. The messiah is one for whom the new 'inner' life could not suffice; he is obsessed by the need for immediate contact with the Absolute; but this is no longer practicable except by conduct. The messiah is a moralist, either religious or political. The Order which the messiah needs to realize, the monk is content to contemplate. But the increasing importance of the political in modern times makes the monk's abstentionism more and more difficult to justify; and yet the monk cannot act without betraying objectivity—his *raison d'être*. The messiah, therefore, attempts to cope with problems rendered doubly acute by the monk's aloofness, while his efforts are often disastrous because they are made in the name of another type of objectivity, one which involves the sacrifice of existence to system.

45

Our scientific culture has therefore evolved two objectivities, that of a supreme Order, not embodied in objects as in Aristotelian physics but concealed in them and which consequently calls into existence a second objectivity, that of an 'inner world' with which to communicate. These two worlds become places of refuge in the sense that the messiah need not think, he is simply bringing existence into line with the Order inherent in it; while the monk need not act since (if he is consistent) he regards Order as capable of establishing itself, the whole duty of man being to devote himself to the inner world of culture, to the development of the self.

If we are able to impugn classical thought, not in its results but in its very nature as we have done, then it can only be because we have reached in our time a great philosophical parting of the ways. Modern art offers the best guarantee we could wish that orthodox philosophies have yielded not to a 'fashion' nor to a crisis of disillusionment and despair but to a cultural reorientation no less important than that which brought scholasticism to an end. Since the renaissance, art has striven to represent the invisible Order posited by scientific thought. The 'great individual' of the renaissance and humanism was not an individual in the sense of differing from others, but in the sense of carrying to perfection an objective ideal—he realized one aspect of cosmic order. With cubism, the artist tries to represent objects as he sees them, not as he knows them to be; and yet he copies reality, since there is no necessary connection between the 'true nature' of an object and, for example, its exact dimensions which the classical painter scrupulously reproduces in scale but which the cubist neglects because that is not what he sees. Mind considered as an objective instrument indispensable to the correct interpretation of the exterior world becomes in this way superfluous because things are what we see them to be. To express this differently: subjectivity which, up until now, has been the source of error becomes that of truth, since appearance is reality itself and not a deceitful veil necessitating the intervention of a mind capable of removing it. Reality is a point of view or orientation, and not a hidden Object.

What all this amounts to in more practical terms, we shall see in a final chapter. We must now look more closely at the arguments with which the objective intellectual usually justifies himself.

II

No one thinks of criticizing a man because he limps. But almost in the same degree a man's religion has come to enjoy a similar immunity. Is this not an admission that religion is unconsciously regarded as a kind of infirmity which it is somehow 'unfair to question'? Not so very many years ago unbelief was an accomplishment, a liberation; today, one is born into it, and belief has become an accomplishment; so that it is no longer the 'ignorant masses' who believe, but the refined. If one avoids questioning a man about his religion, however, it is often less a fear of driving him to a manifest renunciation of his reason (a number of artful dodges usually inspired by the 'collapse of science' have been devised) than a hesitancy to approach the question of motives. Men who became freethinkers did so in many cases in the hope of making themselves more useful to their fellow men. Voltaire no longer has anything to teach us, but he will never cease to merit our admiration and gratitude for having so often expressed himself in this vein: 'You are a great thinker [he wrote to d'Alembert] but it is not enough to show that one is more intelligent than others. Come then, be of some use to humanity.'[1] As far as being concerned about whether or not men are properly fed and educated the Church has not changed much since

[1] If christianity is primarily a religion of mercy and love, then among the greatest christians of modern times are men like Marx and Sartre whose first concern is the welfare of their fellows and not, as is so often the case with the believer, peace of mind.

the eighteenth century (one has only to think of Italy, Spain, Portugal and Ireland) and if a good number of well-educated people have turned back to it, it is certainly not with the expectation of being better placed to serve humanity. Indeed, what is perhaps most admirable in the two noblest of modern catholics—Péguy and Bernanos—whose ferocious contempt for a 'culture' smelling of banknotes we can fully share, is precisely their mistrust of the Church as a *political* institution. Most believers, of course, except the most naïve, do not concern themselves about matters of public well-being because they know full well that religion, if it is a solution, is a solution for the individual; politically it is simply irrelevant. What the convert seeks is to re-establish contact with the 'eternal truths'; he wants peace and is prepared to pay the price—to pretend that the burning problems of the day are no business of his[1] and even that his reason is a kind of 'pride' which he must renounce, although this constitutes a form of self-mutilation more grotesque than those practised by primitive peoples (and one which the communist does not at least make a matter *of principle*, as the apologists of religion often do). If the achievement of spiritual comfort is not to appear a selfish abandonment of the vast majority of men incapable of belief, sincere or hypocritical, then it must be regarded as a struggle to preserve spiritual values in a world given over to materialism. But since religion is ineffectual politically, this amounts to championing the individual against the mass, and we have here the argument which the objective society, including its senior members, the humanists, will never fail to invoke—the necessity of protecting our cultural and spiritual values (that is, the sanctity of the individual) against successive waves of messianic barbarism.

The objective intellectual, of course, often protests against the obscurantism of the believer, but what lies deepest in a man is not his reason, it is what he wants to accomplish with it. We do not use reason to help us make the important choices of our lives; we choose, and reason serves to justify the choice. The religious messiah having ceased to place so much emphasis upon morality, or act, his choice is seen to bear a striking resemblance to that of the monk.

[1] There is, to be sure, the progressive catholicism of *l'Esprit*, but its efforts are as effectively thwarted by Rome (see the affair of the worker priests) as are those of local communisms by marxist dogma. What reforms the Church was capable of, it executed at the time of the counter-reformation—*before* the spirit of free enquiry which is part of the heritage of communism, a heritage with which it will have eventually to come to terms.

The objectivity which the monk will put forth as distinguishing him radically from the believer, on the contrary, converts a resemblance into what is almost an identity. In both cases we have an ethic which not only permits, but enjoins, a passive submission to events which other less 'spiritual' members of the community are left to face unaided. Since partisanship is incompatible with objectivity, the monk is obliged to hold, with the christian, that the powers of light will eventually triumph over those of darkness; we need only be unambiguous about our preference for the former.

The christian already possesses the Truth, so that all his intellectual effort is bent towards *conservation*; but this again is equally true of the monk, except that we are much less clear as to exactly what is being conserved and how.

I fear I shall be criticized for a lack of objectivity in my entire approach to the academic intellectual. From the outset, I have made no attempt to conceal my hostility. But it would have been hypocritical to pretend that after careful examination of the facts, I had been reluctantly led to a certain number of conclusions about university people making a profession of the arts. This does not mean that I am simply engaged in justifying a subjective irritation; it means that, as is always the case with vital issues, the truth does not hide, it strikes us in the face, and the only 'problem' is, are we going to do something about it or are we not. The question is never what is known or not known, but what is proclaimed or kept to ourselves. It is a peculiar characteristic of consciousness to be able to have knowledge of something and simultaneously to deny that it has. This goes further than mere hypocrisy, for we have all at one time or another successfully lied to ourselves; and it is no doubt by this means that the conscientious academic manages to live with himself. He knows that the results of his research are scandalously out of proportion with the time and labour expended, that the best years of his life have been devoted to the writing of something that no one would read even if it were published. What is even more grave, he knows that what he has to offer his students they take, but often with a wry face, because it is said to be good for them, and that they come to him in the first place only because they lacked either the intelligence or the application or both to work for a degree in science. It is difficult for me to believe that even the academic high priest who has published work that filters through to an occasional man in the street can feel much more comfortable than the obscure

49

scholar about the role he plays in society. One has only to contrast the *Encyclopédie* with modern learned journals; indeed, one need only be present for a few moments at a gathering of academics (which resembles nothing so much as a meeting of church elders) to be aware that not only has all enthusiasm departed, but that enthusiasm, which is still sometimes found in American scholars, is treated (and quite rightly of course) with a kind of amused paternal condescension. It is perfectly in order to compare the academic to the *philosophe* rather than to his eighteenth-century counterpart, since the existence, in the age of reason, of a recognized intellectual aristocracy made the medieval stupor in which the universities were plunged a matter of indifference, whereas the modern universities' stupor of scientific objectivity is a catastrophe since we can look nowhere else for intellectual leadership.

All this, I repeat, the academic knows; and what is of great help in enabling him simultaneously not to know it is his isolation from the rest of the community where a hierarchy of persons is established depending more or less upon the number of people whose lives are affected by a given occupation. Even the atomic scientist is not isolated, since his work will eventually have a profound influence upon the daily lives of his fellow citizens. In the case of the academic the gauge of utility does not function, laymen cannot therefore judge him, and an *esprit de corps* prevents any determined criticism from within. It is not altogether accurate to say that the community does not judge its academics, but its judgement is ambiguous; for while its university teachers are poorly paid on the one hand (in their *own* opinion, that is; a miner would not consider them poorly paid), on the other they are numbered among the 'distinguished' members of the social group. In other words, the attitude of the world at large reflects very accurately the state of the intellectual's own mind which at once knows and does not know its utter social inutility.

To this, the academic replies simply that his is the supreme utility, that without which the others are meaningless; he alone is concerned not with the comfort of life, but with its enrichment, its quality. But here we should be cautious, for there is no middle way; either the universities offer the most precious of all commodities, a fuller life, or they have betrayed a charge. Someone has said that it is not the strength of evil we must fear so much as the weakness of what is right. Political crimes, it will be answered, are the outcome of political fanaticism and it is precisely the function of the intellec-

50

tual to pass on the cultural acquisitions of man which alone can give a meaning to life apart from fanaticism. It is the mission of the university to keep in existence a hard core of individuals devoted to the preservation of the 'higher' values which those of the masses are threatening to engulf. How do these individuals acquit themselves?

Here again the academic must not know what he cannot help but know. The scientific approach to the non-scientific is everywhere the practice in universities, but surely there is no one left today who will defend it. A great book is like a piece of music which may be interpreted in a great many different ways depending upon the instrumentalist and the prevailing tastes. The book, like the music, is a challenge to draw from it what we can, and whether the result is what the author or composer intended is of very little importance, even there where it is possible to learn exactly what was intended. But then, how can we be sure that the artist himself knew what he meant; that is, does meaning come before or after the creative act? One of the joys of writing is to discover in a sentence just completed a meaning we did not fully intend but which can be enthusiastically adopted. An author need not wait for the passing of years for his work to become foreign to him, for unless his thought is a commonplace, language does not simply express it, it *helps to fashion it*. Alain remarked that: 'The need to write is the desire to know what one is going to find.' Except perhaps in the case of the messiah, the author himself often discovers as much as he expresses a meaning. Is there any sense, therefore, in denying to subsequent generations the right to discover in their turn? Since the work is exterior to and in part independent of its creator, the view of the intelligent and informed reader can be almost as authoritative as that of the author.

Only the lesser artist can declare himself fully satisfied with his work, because such satisfaction indicates that he has succeeded in 'expressing himself'; that his art is not a further exploration of the real, but a mere recapitulation. The art of 'self-expression' is easily 'perfect', whether because form and idea pre-exist as in a dying classical art, or because it is considered permissible to dispense with both as in minor romanticisms. The great artist whether classic or romantic is perpetually haunted by the possible, of which the 'finished' work is only an approximation. Who expresses 'himself' is in reality restating what his predecessors acquired for him to express, whether idea or emotion; for in what way is the expression of idea less personal than that of emotion, which, unfortunately, is as trans-

51

missible as idea? It is characteristic of humanism to see in a man's greatness a quality rather than an activity; his work as artist or thinker is taken to be the expression of a kind of essence which other men are born without, the objectification of a unique Self. But if a great book is really the adequate projection of a Self, the outward form of a constant and identifiable cause which the literary historian will be able to fix for all time, then we shall be hard put to explain its centuries-long appeal. The great artist or writer produces for his contemporaries, not for the ages, as do the impotent; and it is absurd to suppose that they consciously placed in their works everything that has been found there. The artist has to believe in himself in order to carry on, but this does not preclude moments, often very frequent, during which he turns desperately to others for some assurance that his work is not worthless. The opinion of a fool can deprive him of his sleep, because no man is great for himself. Greatness is an activity whose products are rich with ambiguities, and their creator is often disconcertingly ready to accept an interpretation which *we* propose. And the choice not to propose is not ours to make—the attempt to identify a single objective meaning which will be 'discovered' and not proposed is as subjective an approach as any, and more barren than most. Montaigne and Rabelais were not atheists, but half a century ago the most objective of scholars believed that they were, because until recently scholars were usually atheists. But the mistake of these critics was not to have considered Montaigne and Rabelais atheists—for to have turned as completely as they did from religion as a guide and as a philosophy is a kind of atheism, or at least a long stride toward it— their mistake was to have supposed the evidence for atheism a definitively and objectively acquired fact which, along with a few others, would enable us to attach a final meaning to the work of Montaigne and Rabelais. This busy storing away of precious facts (which offers a curious parallel to the main activity of the acquisitive society—the accumulation of money) in view of a supreme purchase strikes us, after only a generation or two, as a preposterous naïvety, and yet the work goes forward despite the conflict between practice and what must be a general realization of its pointlessness. For what can be the object of an exhaustive investigation into, for example, the sources of *Don Quixote*, of *Phèdre*, of *Tom Jones*, if not to help discover the 'key' to the nature of genius, just as an examination of environment helps explain the appearance of a plant or animal.

Study has been so exclusively concentrated upon 'environment' that the recent tendency to read the texts themselves comes as a rather ingenious innovation. If the purpose of so much fastidious research is not, as it once was (in Taine, for example), to 'explain' genius, then it must be to help us to understand and to enjoy its creations. (Though here it should be remarked at the outset that just as much effort goes into the investigation of authors whose only resemblance to the great of the past is that they also are dead.)

In his *Confessions*, Rousseau wrote: '. . . my talent . . . was less in my pen than in my heart . . .' and this is true of every great talent, the more so in that, as Vauvenargues remarked, 'great thoughts come from the heart'. Style responds to the exigencies of thought, and the lesser writer is one of whom the reverse may be said. The age of reason was at the same time one of superb style—Hume, Swift, Gibbon, Voltaire, Montesquieux, etc. One is not aware of a great style, it is a transparent medium, and when it begins to grow opaque, the author is 'understood', we have absorbed his thought, and except for a particularly incisive insight here and there, only the style remains. Everyone is familiar with the anecdote of the French noblewoman who, about to go out for the evening, picked up a copy of *La Nouvelle Héloïse* and was unable to put it down again. What held this woman enraptured was not Rousseau's language, it was a conception of love very different from that of restoration comedy and of *Les Liaisons Dangereuses* or, at best, of Marivaux, which had prevailed for so long. But romantic love has gone hideously to seed in the women's magazines and it is a great scholar indeed who can read *La Nouvelle Héloïse* from beginning to end however much he admires the style. We may be sure that the men responsible for the King James version of the Bible were not intent upon creating 'literature', for this is one of the conditions of the creation of great literature. The dissociation of content and style is therefore a betrayal; but admittedly it is one that is inevitable because the greater the author, the less that will remain of him in addition to style, which is like a bone from which the generations have gnawed the meat. The greatest compliment we can pay a classic is to find it a bore—the greatness of Beethoven's fifth symphony lies in the fact that we can no longer listen to it. *Hamlet* is a 'collection of old quotations', and what the scholars preserve, therefore, is not Shakespeare, but John Lyly. A cultural heritage that has to be preserved is not worth preserving, for what is really vital in it will have become part of us. Men like Bacon, Montaigne, Voltaire, have helped fashion the typical western European mentality, and to make these thinkers the objects of an alleged impersonal scientific study is a kind of intellectual narcissism in which only the weary can take pleasure. There are no 'discoveries' to be made in such authors; they may be re-interpreted, but the only important reinterpretation will be part of an attempt to *utilize* them in the construction of the future. This can be irritating, as it is in the marxist messiah; but the marxist need not be a messiah. If partisan studies of great authors are often infuriating, those of the monk are ludicrous. I have before me a huge volume of five hundred large closely printed pages entitled *La Religion de Voltaire*. In its conclusion, one reads: '. . . from one end to the other of that long life, Voltaire was ardently and aggressively a deist.' One need not read much of Voltaire to learn this; or, for that matter, does it even have to be consciously learned. It may not be common knowledge that there could be an ardour in deism, but what is important about deism is precisely that it was so rarely ardent. The amassing of information about great writers could once be exciting because it was to have led to an understanding of what was 'behind' the process of literary creation. But with the disappearance of scientific zeal we are thrown back from what 'caused' them to the works themselves; and here, since the essential is understood, we must invent 'problems' which only exhaustive research will solve. Let me recall a well-known philosophical problem: if we place both our hands, one cold and the other warm, into a pan of water, how can we know whether the water is cold or warm since it will feel cold to one hand and warm to the other? There is no 'problem' here, unless we hypothesize in the person involved a degree of ignorance of his surroundings which could not exist apart from an artificial isolation. The 'problems' of literary history are often of the same kind, they require an artificially created ignorance in exchange for which one is led to hidden truths. Thus, we cannot simply accept what genius unambiguously teaches, we must look for influences and motivations. This is what constitutes true understanding. Knowing more about an author than about what he said has a double advantage—in the case of the classics, what was said is no longer of any interest because it has been incorporated into our ways of thought, and in the case of contemporaries or near contemporaries, we are able to ignore the summons to act or to change our ways which is sounded in every really great book. To appreciate the

54

extent to which objectivity has become, like religion, a refuge from constructive activity, one need only consider that there is no more effective way of emasculating a book than to make it the subject of research; there is no more effective way of ignoring what D. H. Lawrence has to say about sex than to enquire into why he says it. Broad-mindedness costs the scholar nothing, for scholarship has become a device for dealing with unpleasant truths without having to act upon them, since (and I cannot return too frequently to this point) one cannot act without violating objectivity. Péguy's enemies, the *sorbonnards*, have wreaked a terrible vengeance because, as Péguy himself gloomily foresaw, they have turned his writings into thesis fodder. The detachment with which the Anglo-Saxon intellectual in particular encounters truth is, given the present state of the world, a terrifying phenomenon. To be able to make an 'objective' study of men like Stendhal, Nietzsche, Gide or Sartre is to betray a barbarism more sinister than that of total ignorance. Objectivity runs risks that increase in proportion to the relevance and timeliness of the question at hand; no scholar, therefore, likes to pronounce upon an issue until time has brought about a general accord, until it has become possible to substitute information (contemplation) for intelligence (act). This is one of the reasons for which the intellectual always has a word of gentle understanding for a long-dead author, however inconsequential, but none for a living author, however great. The intellectual is 'frankly disappointed' by his contemporaries who, once they are dead, will become the objects of painstaking research. Confronted by the present, the first concern of the intellectual is not to decide what action ought to be taken, who denounced and who supported, it is to *seek a precedent*, and having found one he conjures the possibility of enthusiasm. It is interesting to note the irritation one provokes in academic circles by suggesting that something is new; by suggesting, for example, that modern poetry, art and philosophy are different in kind from the poetry, art and philosophy we are familiar with, and that our ancient definitions are in urgent need of revision. The fact that no really compelling historical precedents can be found for many aspects of modern culture does not disturb the monk who simply names such anomalies 'fashions'. When the danger of enthusiasm has passed, when the 'fashion' no longer solicits a decision or an act, it is transformed into a 'movement', passes into the history books, becomes a precedent, and excites heated discus-

55

sions. The ideas of an author are rarely considered for the aid they may bring us in our present dilemmas, but only as part of a historical sequence or tradition, and to understand an idea is to know where it came from, never how it could be put to use. The refusal to consider an idea in itself, apart from its historical context, that is, for its value as a tool with which we might cut into reality, not only protects it from a biased exploitation by the messiah, but also from a more intelligent utilization by anyone else.

The academic is one for whom our cultural and historical past can have no significance, for if it had he would be offering his students interpretations of facts and ideas, and not the facts and ideas themselves in a shapeless heap, a technique which is sometimes referred to as 'treating the student like an adult'. I believe this refusal on the part of the academic intellectual to attach a meaning to the past (a meaning which will give our society a direction without committing it to a fanaticism) is a refusal of responsibility which students more or less explicitly resent. When I first took up a university post, I remember being shocked by the lack of sympathy between teachers and the mass of the students whose almost total lack of responsiveness was a source of continual and bitter complaint. It was universally assumed, however, that the fault lay in the stomach and never in the food 'submitted' to it,[1] which was that much more odd in that the more honest of my colleagues were always ready to admit that their profferings were in part indigestible. But even when they were not, the objective approach deprived them of whatever power to nourish they might have had. To teach, for example, Voltaire 'objectively', is to treat him as a historical curiosity. To fail to present his work as a great stride away from religious intolerance and obscurantism (which unhappily is still very much with us) is to betray both Voltaire and the student.[2] Voltaire can only be alive for us to the extent in which

[1] The academic always 'submits', he never insists, given the possibility that this be interpreted not as narrow-minded obstinacy (which would be perfectly safe) but as a sufficiently strong *conviction* to make him seek to persuade or to oppose; and in matters that are not trivial this is known as 'corrupting the youth'.

[2] In this perspective, the next great figure of literary history would be Stendhal, who knew that eighteenth-century rationalism was a permanent acquisition and that attempts to defend the religious and social values of the *ancien régime* had brought into being one of the great characteristics of the nineteenth century, its hypocrisy. Ours is a period of defence, if not of restoration as was that of Stendhal, and the only way to 'get on' is to pretend (like a hero of Stendhal) that one accepts the old order. If one is a philosopher one's position will be 'essentially that of Hume' (as one of our philosophers has written), the historian will believe in the divine mission of Christianity (instead of that of the proletariat) and

we accept his ideas as a *progress*, not toward some final goal, but in the general direction of the liberation of the human from the non-human, toward the suppression of one form of what was to be called man's alienation. Students who are most worth troubling about are those in whom the brainwashing of church and newspaper has not been altogether successful and who therefore come to the University looking for some means of interpreting the world about them.[1] But this they will not be offered. They may be encouraged to 'think for themselves', but the most original of thinkers is always deeply in-debted to others, even the best student needs a point of departure, he needs to be encouraged to adopt a point of view from which things will fall into some kind of perspective, from which they will begin to make sense. But things can only make sense in so far as they are made to suggest certain *possibilities of action*; the only way to 'understand' a saw is to know how to use it. The same applies to the world in which we live; 'in itself', 'objectively', it is nothing. In the neatly labelled parcels of learning offered to him by the modern university, the student will find no indication of what is to be done. He must therefore either go away empty-handed (except that he will have 'prepared' himself to teach) or stay behind to brood over our immense unproductive capital of information. As a scholar he will be a gentleman, and academic freedom will be granted without the slightest fear of its being abused. In some cases, he may even be free to become a marxist; but, as we have seen, orthodox marxism, that is, marxism as a form of scientism (which it need not be), is 'objec-tive' and therefore involves the existence of a 'regular clergy', the academic interpreters of the law, who will not be much closer to making their weight felt than are their colleagues, since act will follow from principle rather than from the requirements of a given political or economic situation.[2] The marxist has found his 'law',

everyone except the messiah will be 'objective', that is, neither of our age nor of our society, yet in some mysterious way not non-existent.

[1] One has to read students' essays to appreciate the uniformity of thought about vital issues (or for that matter about any other) that exists in the 'free world'. I find it hard to believe that it is any more complete among, for example, Chinese students. There is, however, an important difference. The Chinese, with their uniformity, are performing prodigies, while we, with ours, are not even able to hold our own.

[2] The academic marxist who is not an 'absolutist' is no better placed for effective action because he is the partisan of a philosophy which must be revised in the light of events if it is to regain widespread allegiance. One of the few philosophers of stature who has given this question the attention it deserves is Sartre. But more of that later.

the monk is still, theoretically, seeking his; in both cases, act is considered to be dependent upon thought and the tragic division of men into those who do and those who 'think' is perpetuated.

The monk has had time to forget that his objectivity, deriving as it does from science, is identical with that of the marxist messiah, the only difference being that the monk is more logical since he sees the superfluousness of act if man's destiny is not in his own keeping, or if it depends upon the uncovering of nature's 'secrets'. The monk will therefore argue that his objectivity has nothing to do (as I maintain) with standing aside so as to permit the untrammelled functioning of 'law'; its purpose is to preserve as intact as possible the cultural acquisitions of the race, which are a good in themselves apart from interpretations in view of effective action (as opposed to the action of the marxist scientist, which is apt to be abortive because it is dictated by principle rather than need). The understanding as opposed to the interpretation of the past requires no practical justification since it is in this way that life is made worth living, in this way that the accomplishments of the past become cultural enrichment, self-aggrandizement, aesthetic enjoyment. Again, we are dealing with a 'higher' utility than that of which I have been speaking.

We have been concerned with understanding in the sense of the absorption of meaning. We come now to understanding in the sense of 'understanding an epoch' so as to be able to enjoy its literary and artistic productions as did the men of the period. The more we know about Elizabethan fashions in dress or the favourite reading of the English gentry at the beginning of the last century, the better we shall be able to appreciate Shakespeare or Coleridge.

Is not sympathy, however, in the sense of intellectual and moral assent more vital here than understanding? It is not very difficult to understand sexual morality as Richardson envisaged it, but is it possible to sympathize with it to the extent of enjoying *Pamela*? And if so, how could the same reader sympathize with Fielding? It is painfully clear that to be well endowed for his work the objective scholar must be incapable of deeply felt intellectual or moral convictions, otherwise how could he hope to put a literary work into its setting so successfully as to be able to enjoy it? How could he hope to appreciate both Milton and Sterne, both Hemingway and Virginia Woolf, both Gide and Barrès?[1] One of the consequences of

[1] In his book on Héloïse and Abélard (Hollis and Carter, 1953, p. 78) Etienne Gilson tries to persuade us that at this point in their correspondence Héloïse is

this state of affairs is that the voluntary reading of the majority of our university students probably differs little from that of the person who has never had the 'advantages of a university education'.

The astonishing thing about this historical method of literary appreciation is that no one ever feels called upon to defend it. It is as though nothing could be more natural. However, a number of years ago, I remember coming upon a defence of literary research in Jean Pommier's published lecture entitled *Paul Valéry and Literary Creation*. M. Pommier lectures at the Collège de France; he is therefore one of the high priests of the profession and we are justified in attaching a particular importance to his words. He refers to Valéry as having said somewhere that we know little or nothing of the lives of Homer and Shakespeare, and that all this ignorance is not in the least detrimental to our enjoyment of their poetry. Valéry remarks also: 'Accumulate as many details as you are able on the life of Racine, you will not find in them the secret of his art.' (Biographical research is not the whole of literary research, but it is probably the greater part of it, especially if we consider how closely it is related to the study of influences and sources.) M. Pommier fixes upon the second of Valéry's observations and has no trouble in showing that we learn something of the genesis of Racine's art in examining bits of literary theorizing which have come down to us from a certain Lemaitre of whom Racine was for a while the pupil. M. Pommier has side-stepped the issue by confusing information about a work of art with enjoyment of it; he asserts that the two go together, he does not prove it. It has been my experience that aesthetic enjoyment may well decrease in proportion with the increase of one's information. M. Pommier mentions Gerard de Nerval's *Chimères*. It was discovered a few years ago that a dictionary of alchemy had played a large role in the composition of these poems. However much intellectual enjoyment this discovery may have afforded the specialists, I do not see how it can fail to detract

wrong in resisting her husband's attempts to recall her to greater piety and Abélard right. Few of us however still live in the twelfth century and it is precisely the divine earthliness of Héloïse which endears her to us, does honour to her sex and makes these letters still readable. To side wholeheartedly with Abélard on this issue would be to turn the most beautiful passages of Héloïse's letters into the scandalous vagaries of an insubordinate woman. If we followed the logic of the scholar, we should take toward Stendhal the attitude of his contemporaries— we should ignore him. The scholar who sympathizes with both Abélard and Héloïse, both Chateaubriand and Stendhal is not being objective, he is killing literature.

59

from the delicate and unique charm of some of Nerval's sonnets. He himself remarked that *Les Chimères* would lose their charm upon being explained, if it were possible to do so. Poets like Nerval, Coleridge (in poems like Kubla Khan), Baudelaire, Mallarmé, Valéry, Eliot were striving to divorce poetry from meaning, they sought to make it *evocative*. The fact that poetry in a foreign language which we still have difficulty in translating will often seem finer than it is, indicates a dependence of poetic effect upon a certain mistiness of meaning.[1] The literary scholar appears to be engaged in translating poetry into prose, and prose into poetry.

At the basis of the whole question of the preservation of culture lies this confusion between the enjoyment involved in gathering ever more information about a given subject (in no way different from the pleasure of, for example, the stamp collector) and aesthetic enjoyment properly speaking. If the two become one, as is sometimes said, in the higher reaches of mathematics, they remain easily distinguishable in the field of research into literature and art; indeed, when one thinks of the learned journals one is inclined to consider them as being hopelessly incompatible. A good example of this failure to distinguish between enjoyment of and information about is the study of folk music as it has survived in various parts of the world. One can understand how the recording of old English ballads in the Kentucky hills could be of great interest for the musicologist, but from there to enjoying the high-pitched wail of one of these singers is a great step. It would be dangerous to reply here that this music is too far removed from us for our interest in it to be anything but historical, for must not the same thing be said of *Beowolf*, of *La Chanson de Roland*, of medieval art in its entirety, and of how much other art down almost to the present? It would be equally pointless to reply that some of this old music survives in modern form and is still widely enjoyed, because what the scholar aims at is an objective restitution of the past and not only is this an impossibility, but the past can only survive in so far as we make use of it just as the ballads survive only in so far as they assume a modern form. It may well be that ballad hunters enjoy the music they record, but I insist that for the greater part of such music the distinction between the pleasure of the collector and aesthetic enjoyment is to be made. This distinction is not an artificial one because it is essen-

[1] That this should not be true of the poetry of Pope proves simply that the nature of poetry has changed since the eighteenth century.

tially that which we make between learning and culture. Anyone who has moved in academic circles knows that not only can great learning be divorced from culture, it frequently is. 'Culture' is one of those peculiar words which no one seems to be able to define satisfactorily and yet which we bestow upon certain individuals or withhold from them with a completely justified assurance. Someone has said that culture is what remains after one has forgotten everything, and this is true in the sense that the cultivated man does not store up learning, he utilizes it in the creation of a better life, and if culture is disappearing, it is partly because it has been entrusted to the objective scholar who in order to be 'objective' deliberately divorces himself from life.

I have been arguing that aesthetic enjoyment is too often confused with the pleasure involved in gathering information about the past. There is, however, another respect in which the 'beauty' of an object would seem to consist in something extraneous to it—like information about it—and that is age. A striking example of this is the recent revival of interest in, of all things, Victorian architecture. But to appreciate the full importance of this question, one needs to ponder upon Malraux's disconcerting remark: 'If the Victory of Samothrace were discovered to be a fake, it would be completely destroyed for us. But if it were discovered to be a fifteenth-century fake, its destruction would be less radical.' There have been times when the age of a work of art had a tendency to make it meaningless and therefore ugly; today the reverse would appear to be true— beauty depends upon the absence of meaning and therefore in many cases upon great antiquity. The ugly (modern art) is precisely what is replete with meaning; except that in some circles the absurdity of condemning a great artistic movement to ugliness is avoided through recourse to formal values.

In addition to M. Pommier, T. S. Eliot, in *Points of View*, defends the existing system, and on two grounds. First, the labours of the scholars make possible the flights of the great critics. The test of a great critic, however, is that he be able to identify in a work that part of it most independent of historical or biographical fact. The difference between the great and the lesser critic is the difference between the cultivated and the learned man. The merely learned critic will rarely be able to pass an accurate judgement upon his contemporaries, because his concern is to situate historically; but art, like language, makes its own rules, and the critic who is merely

61

learned will always be, like the grammarians, several generations or so behind. The great critic, to be sure, will also be a man of considerable learning, but his judgement of a book would have been substantially the same in the absence of any information about it. We judge a piece of furniture upon its serviceableness, and this is also the most reliable method of judging a work of art. Those worn-out works of art which we call classics are, like old furniture, put aside and admired for their 'form' or their style, but the craftsman intended them to be sat upon. Our academics are fussy antiquarians who consider that they perform a vital service in trying unsuccessfully to convert the youth of the nation to antiquarianism. We have seen that prose which no longer has anything to teach is transformed by the guardians of our culture into art, but other creative activities seek also to teach, in the wider sense of 'interpretation', and when an interpretation is thoroughly understood, we have the art of the museums. It is easy to imagine a successful Van Meegeren who would have produced not merely new Vermeers, but new Rembrandts. He would nevertheless have remained a simple counterfeiter, for the greatness of an artist is his vision, not his technique; and the vision of Rembrandt is no longer the conquest of a bold mind, it is there for anyone to take. If we are to admire the primitives, we must, as does Berenson, admire them for their formal values. But I cannot help feeling that this is, at least in part, another example of the confusion between the pleasure of knowing (that of the specialist) and aesthetic enjoyment; not to mention the fact that one runs the risk of applying to modern art a vocabulary evolved for an earlier art and missing the point altogether as does Berenson. The art of the past has subsided into a technique because its interpretations are worn out. The lesson of modern art is still to be learned, but there is no point in looking to the scholar for help; what is needed is thought about what is going on in the world around us *at this moment*; and for the scholar, all that is an appearance which only historical perspective will change into reality. The great critic is not one who has absorbed the work of the scholars; the scholar is interested in facts about a work, the good critic is concerned with its 'serviceableness'. What does *Axel's Castle*, for example, owe to the learned journals? As for the more remote past, the only great criticism will involve a reinterpretation in view of a future we wish to construct; and for this, the works themselves suffice. Even if the objective restoration of the past at which the scholar aims were possible, there would remain the problem of interpretation, of attaching a significance; there would remain a complex of prejudice, desire, ambition, which would produce a variety of interpretations, and the work of the scholar is to see to the establishment of the least selfish and the most constructive. Apart from this, the function of the classic is to turn adolescents into adults, to enable them to 'catch up' with the age in which they live. Aesthetic enjoyment appears to me absolutely inseparable from an enlargement of the understanding, from an increased capacity to deal effectively with life; and the intensity of pleasure with which we read Cervantes or Keats when we are seventeen will never again be equalled, unless we have the good fortune later on to encounter and to be able to understand a contemporary with a new 'vision,' with something new to teach us.

Eliot's second argument in defence of historical research is one which no doubt most scholars would put forward if questioned upon the matter. The bare facts, according to Eliot, cannot corrupt taste, it is 'opinion and fancy' that does this. Such is the principle of historical objectivity and we should expect Eliot to have a kind word for it, since the practical effect of objectivity, whatever the intention, is always to bolster the status quo, and for those for whom the good life is inseparable from occidental religion and culture this is a vital matter at a time when the tiny peninsular of Europe, for so long the head of the vast Eurasian continent, is rapidly becoming its tail. We must suppose that the 'taste' which Eliot is anxious to preserve is one of which he has given examples in his critical work, and while it is in excellent taste to admire

In sua voluntate è nostra pace

not merely for the poetry but also, and perhaps even mainly, for the sentiment, it is a sentiment one is tempted to cite as an example of an 'opinion and fancy' which, applied to modern literature, could corrupt taste. Objectivity, when it is not inconsequential, in other words when it is patently not objective, is the recourse of those at odds with their times. It precludes participation. It is inevitably backward-looking and nostalgic, because it is inevitably 'discovery', never creation.[1] One cannot be objective about the future, which we

[1] The fact that Eliot is modern in his poetry and 'medieval' in his thought illustrates the way in which an artist and his work may go different ways. Eliot's poetry exists, so to speak, in spite of him. Somewhat the same applies to the work of writers like François Mauriac and Graham Greene, from whose novels

desire to be this or that. The objective critic is one who has sought a refuge in the past under the pretext of discovering there some principle of guidance. But he will only discover what he himself puts there. The theory of 'unified sensibility' does not spring unaided from the facts. Eliot conceived the theory and selected the facts necessary to support it; and the only way to avoid subjectivity of this kind is to select the facts in function of a future which not we alone, but most people either want or should want. But this brings up questions which I shall attempt to deal with later.

Modern scholarship in the arts falls between two stools—it is neither science nor humanism. The renaissance humanist, if he was a good one, aimed at much more than a sound knowledge of Greek, Latin and Hebrew. He was concerned with the formation of better men, the philosopher prince, the Cortegiano, or the young man fashioned by the sort of education Montaigne advocates. The scientific study of our cultural past is kept going by its own momentum; the conviction has long since gone out of it, and the academic will usually fall back upon talk of 'culture'. I have tried to show, however, that the academic's conception of an 'objective' past, of a 'self-contained', quasi-autonomous past, which is therefore to be *learned*, is incompatible with the idea of culture which, however we define it, unquestionably has something to do with the quality of life, something to do with the interpretation as opposed to the mere learning of fact. But if the universities refuse their students an interpretation of the world, it is not only out of concern for objectivity, it is because culture as commonly understood is indissolubly associated with the individual in so far as he stands aside from the masses, in so far as he resists complete integration. He does not therefore require an interpretation of the world because his function is not to act but to conserve, not to propose, but to oppose, and Trilling has aptly used the expression 'opposing self'. So we return to this other objectivity of which I spoke in the last chapter—the self considered as object rather than as act. Just as objectivity as respect for the facts derives from science as a quest for the absolute object (or what Meyerson called 'identity') so the opposing self derives from the divine self, the objective self of renaissance tragedy and of European aristocracy as it existed down to the French revolution.

we not only can in some cases, but should, draw totally different conclusions from those intended by the author. This is why the great critic can be independent of the scholar—it is the work itself that counts, not what its creator intended.

Today, thinking in our part of the world exists exclusively by opposition to stalinism. Thus we have 'pluralism', which instead of being an attempt to rethink government in the light of contemporary history is simply a restatement of democratic principles offered as an edifying contrast to communist totalitarianism. In the same way, revulsion from dictatorial interference with private life has brought about the rediscovery of the preciousness of the individual as a corrective to mass behaviour and mass values. Such is the ideological gift of the West to the rest of the world: freedom of speech to those who can neither read nor write, the dignity of the individual to people who live half-naked in the shadow of famine. As for the material gifts, no one is grateful for charity but only for instruction as to how to become independent of charity, and capitalism is of no help in a situation where intense overall planning is absolutely indispensable.

For the moment, however, what it is important to remark is that the western individual, while opposing integration on the Russian and Chinese models, not only accepts the herd values of his own society,[1] but has invented psycho-analysis to prevent him from straying from them. Here is a remarkable example of how 'objectivity' works in a society of 'individuals'. The stresses that modern life often produce in sensitive and intelligent people are no longer considered to call for a change in society; it is the individual who is wrong, and he consequently becomes a neurotic, not a revolutionary. No more remarkable device than psycho-analysis has ever been devised by a society for preventing its superior citizens from giving it pain. Even when, as in the case of a Karen Horney, the values of a society are disapproved of, it is suggested that the best course open to the individual is to conform, to integrate himself with the mass, to accept. If he follows the advice of a Moreno, he will learn to 'play roles' adapted to the types of company he keeps, and so become a nonentity several times over rather than only once. Happiness in our individualistic society has come to consist in being as much like other people as possible. During the Korean war, the Chinese managed to convert to communism a few American prisoners who, upon their return home, were treated as mental cases. This,

---

[1] The intellectual, to be sure, deplores the taste and the thinking of the masses, but he accepts them nevertheless inasmuch as the only hope of change lies in constructive political thought, and here the thinking of the intellectual is no better than, in fact it is sometimes inferior to that of the masses.

surely, is to be numbered among the great achievements of science; in the past men could only believe that their enemies were mistaken or corrupt, they can now look upon them as abnormal or insane. But let us turn from the individual as a scientific object to the individual as a repository of cultural values, to the 'opposing self' strong enough to judge society and to refuse to be judged by it.

There is no intellectual vice more common than the failure to see the forest for the trees. In this matter of the cultivated individual (in the classical sense of a person who lives on a higher spiritual level than others), no one cares to see that he was the product of a given social arrangement and of a given historical context and that his time has gone by. Culture, in fact, is inseparable from social responsibility, and while it is possible to direct history, it is impossible to hold it still or push it backwards, yet this is what the universities are attempting in so far as they make it their purpose to improve life by improving the individual as such, in other words by enriching the content of the self.

The christian talks of what a pleasant world this would be if everyone were a good christian, and the practical impossibility of this does not seem to worry him. The academic trying to spread culture as a way of life is in the same position, he is offering a commodity for which there is no longer any demand on a significant scale. This is the cruel fact we must start from, for we shall get further by co-operating with history than by either forcing it to co-operate with us like the messiah or by noting facts about it like the monk.

Our conception of culture is one appropriate to the society which produced the renaissance tragic hero, one for which there existed a class of individuals differing in essence from others, possessing a well-defined objective self with whose fate was mixed up the fate of everyone. Duty to oneself was at the same time duty to mankind. The self was an aspect of cosmic order, an 'election' which one could not refuse—rags do not disguise the nobleman for he ennobles his rags. This divine self could only be betrayed in the most exceptional circumstances, circumstances brought about by divine intervention, by the 'hidden god' of tragedy. There were other types of great individuals; men who, remarkable for their learning or virtue, were able to exercise a real influence upon those around them, not merely as noble examples, but as intercessors. We have made of Prospero a figure of poetry, but he was much more for Shake-

66

speare's contemporaries; and until quite recently, the village boy who with immense industriousness succeeded in educating himself was a source of pride to his community. Unfortunately or not, learning and virtue no longer impress us; they have both become too easy. What many admire in the man of learning is not his knowledge but his leisurely work and his high standard of living; what we admire in the oppressed is not their resignation but their determination to resist. We must not conclude that learning is no longer looked upon as a good in itself and that it once was. What has happened is that we no longer regard learning as an attribute of some inherent greatness, as in the case of the refined aristocrat or the person with a divine mission; nor do we regard it as creative of greatness as did the Stoics. Learning, that is to say, has dissociated itself from the exemplary individual; it has fallen into the public domain, and since its value is no longer guaranteed by the prestige of him who exercises it, then it must be guaranteed by something else, and I fail to see what that can be if not practical achievement. The modern sage is apt to be simply an eccentric and if he is ever again to play a useful role in society, he must learn to be wise in action rather than in meditation. Being no longer a model, he must learn to be a participant. It was once believed that a man was somehow better for knowing his Tacitus, that the study of the classical languages 'improved the mind'. But if one who specializes in, for example, the study of Russian history is not having his mind improved, if he is not becoming a better individual, then why does he take the trouble? It cannot be to make himself more useful to society, because an attempt to utilize his knowledge would destroy his reputation as a scholar.

The disintegration of the divine self was the progress of democracy, and if we are really to invest sovereignty in the people then the individual can no longer be self-sufficient. He can content himself with a refined opposition if he wishes, but the only way to avoid being trampled to death by a stampeding mob is to run ahead trying to guide it past the obstacles. One can look on, of course, from a safe distance, except that no distance is any longer safe. The individual has ceased to count as an example; he exists now only as the representative of a group, and the intellectual has the choice of representing the smallest of these groups, that of the 'cultivated', or the largest, that of his fellow citizens as a whole and ultimately of mankind itself. The concept of the individual existing in and for himself is derived from an aristocratic society in which existence was its own justification and in which therefore leisure was not a period of rest and recreation, but the very stuff of life. In other words, the *individual made culture*, not culture the individual. Let us look more closely at this.

To recall in memory is to embellish; childhood and youth are precious only in retrospect, and this is true of culture which is the memory of a race or civilization. The more remote the event the more easily it is transformed into something of irreplaceable value, and for centuries culture meant simply a knowledge of Latin and Greek. Neither Leonardo nor Michelangelo were 'cultivated' men, they were the mere creators of what would eventually be called culture. Culture, like happiness, is unconscious of itself, otherwise it is no more than a memory. We must therefore make this distinction: there is culture as an act, unconscious of itself because its primary concern is what I have called serviceableness, and there is culture in the sense of a spiritual heritage making up the essential of the 'good life'.

What confuses the issue here is the fact that much of our greatest literature was serviceable to the extent in which it *amused* a tiny oligarchy, for whom passing the time was a major problem. 'If only I could give you my experience!' wrote Madame de Maintenon in one of her letters, 'if only I could describe to you the ennui that devours the great, and the trouble they have to fill their time.'[1] Art was a *commodity* supplied to the great by craftsmen commissioned for the purpose, and when the great themselves took a hand in literature it was as a distraction, much as they might have played chess. A La Rochfoucauld, a Retz, a Saint-Simon, even a Congreve, would have been surprised and probably humiliated to have learned that they would one day come to be more highly esteemed as authors than as noblemen or gentlemen. We must not imagine Montaigne as centering his life in his library and his writing, seeking refuge there from the horrors and stupidities of the time. 'My trade and my art is living,' he writes, and in his essay entitled Of Books, he explains that he only has recourse to reading when he is bored with doing nothing. This consequently is the origin of the Essays which began as simple annotations in the margins of books.

Great artists and writers are of two kinds (as Valéry somewhere remarks), those who are created by a public and those who create a

---

[1] In one of his sermons, Massillon wrote that the life of the great was no more than '. . . a painful precaution against boredom'.

public. I do not believe the latter type, of which examples would be Stendhal, Baudelaire and the cubists, existed before the nineteenth century because before that time there was only one public, only one conceivable public, of which therefore art was a dispensation, a self-projection, whose purest expression was the portrait of the noble-man, which by now may have found its way into a picture gallery but which was intended to be primarily a likeness. It used to be said that Racine's *Bérénice* was inspired by one of Louis XIV's love affairs; in Titus, however, *le roi soleil* would not have seen a figure 'greater than life', but the mere reflection of a divine original. By the time of romanticism the situation was precisely the reverse, art had become a kind of religion, like so much else during that distracted century. The prehegelian mentality was one for which the world was static; one for which there was no becoming. The artist had only to represent what was, and had no need to trouble himself about what might have been. The hegelian Absolute is one that achieves consciousness of itself in time, and art is one of the means it adopts to this end. The artist therefore is engaged in a kind of creation in the sense of a realization; he ceased to be an employee of society and became its judge. The servant of the aristocracy became the scourge of the bourgeoisie. Art was no longer a pastime but a quest for the Absolute. Emma Bovary sought to make her life resemble art—under the *ancien régime* art had resembled life, the forms of which were unchangeable.

Classicism is the tranquil celebration of an unquestioned Order. Reason, as in Molière, is acceptance. But with the end of the eighteenth century, to reason meant to contest, because privilege is irrational. The most remarkable characteristic of bourgeois government throughout the nineteenth century was the radical separation of theory from practice. Theoretically, men were free and equal, practically, the old relationship of master to slave not only continued to exist but was aggravated by the fiction of 'free consent'; the slave was such because he chose to be, and the master was consequently absolved of all responsibility. Under the *ancien régime*, the poet's fulsome dedications to his patron, which we find to be in such bad taste, could be sincere because they were addressed not only to the person but to the institution. In the army, recruits are sometimes encouraged to salute properly by being told that it is the uniform for which they are required to show respect and not the individual. The nobleman symbolized the divine Order as the uniform symbolizes the nation; but the bourgeois symbolized nothing more inspiring than the stock exchange. There is little joy in the possession of privileges which not only can be but are being perpetually challenged, and the bourgeois is desperately anxious to legitimatize his power. To do so he can appeal neither to divine right nor to reason. What he needs is a divine right that can be *acquired*, and this is the role of culture. If the wealthy man cannot ennoble himself, he can nevertheless cultivate himself. Culture is the bourgeois' patent of nobility. In theory anyone can accede to it (it is therefore 'democratic'), and yet it somehow changes a man in essence, as wealth does not. It makes of a *parvenu* a legitimate ruler, and this is what I meant by saying that while at one time the individual made culture, culture now makes the individual.

The nineteenth-century's quest for an Absolute was at the same time an attempt to find a new definition of man, and it has failed. The tragic hero was man in the absolute and conflict took place within himself; the novel, on the other hand, is the art form in which differing conceptions of man confront one another. In an aristocratic society, a bad ruler is none the less a legitimate one. What he does, does not affect what he is. But the bourgeois, whose place is contested by nobler types—the artist, the scientist, the worker—must perform a service, and this he accomplishes by appointing himself the guardian of a cultural heritage. Those who seek to overthrow the régime are ipso facto enemies of culture. The bourgeois is the exact equivalent of what he owns. The prince could not 'exploit' his people because he was always something more and greater than his person; but with the bourgeois to act is to exploit, and he wishes therefore to be associated not with what he does, but with what he possesses.

The most casual examination of art and literature since the French revolution makes it clear that this conception of culture as something that accumulates like capital to enrich the self, to give a kind of legitimacy to class distinctions which were supposed to have been abolished, is the very reverse of culture in the true sense, culture as an activity, as something of which one *makes use*.[1] Both folk and aristocratic art are like those chants that men engaged in some

---

[1] This is clearest in primitive art, where the notion 'art' does not even exist for those who practise it. The Greek word *Agathos* meant beautiful, good and brave in war. Our culture however, in typical rationalist fashion, has effected a division which blinds us to the real nature of art, which is an act, a tool or whatever one wishes except an end in itself; which is to say, except a matter for the individual.

heavy labour sing in unison. Such music is 'entertainment', but without it the work would be unendurable. These arts grow spontaneously from the needs of a group—again, the artist is a product of his public. For the past one hundred and fifty years or so, the reverse has been true. With very few exceptions, the great artist or writer has been the one who refused to conform, one whose art was a protest; and conversely, some of the worst art ever produced has been that of which the dominant social group could fully approve. This is so true that we are suspicious of art that is at once pleasing, and we find it hard to imagine a great artist who would not be misunderstood or neglected by his contemporaries. We can go further and remark that before the nineteenth century it was the philosopher who was in conflict with the established order, and that since the revolution the philosophers, with a few exceptions such as Marx and Nietzsche, have ceased entirely to oppose; their role which is to call into question having been assumed by artists and writers. It might be profitable to look into the reasons for this remarkable development which in more recent times has resulted in an attempt by philosophy (in so far as it is existentialist) to attain truth, in part at least, through literature.

The task of eighteenth-century rationalism was to bring social and religious thought into line with reality. Feudalism had irreparably decayed and the educated classes had turned away from the Church. The problem was to sweep away ideas which no longer commanded the consent of thinking people. After 1789 the situation had been exactly reversed; the question now was how to bring reality into line with the social and religious thought which after the revolution enjoyed popular support. The *philosophes* had to alter theory to suit practice, the revolutionary wanted to change practice so that it might conform to theory. The Declaration of the Rights of Man is as valid now as it was a century and a half ago, and the nineteenth-century revolutionary was not seeking to supplant bourgeois ideology as much as he was trying to implement it. There was in the aristocrat an accord between his thinking and his acting denied the bourgeois, in whom the contrast between what was said and what was done could be grotesque. In all the interminable history of man's cruelty to man, I doubt one will find anything much more atrocious than the early factory system because it involved systematic cruelty to *children*, entirely apart from the way in which particular overseers conducted themselves. But even more serious, if possible, was the

71

decisive demonstration furnished by nineteenth-century capitalism that, contrary to what the Age of Reason had supposed, there was no necessary connection between a man's social and political ideology and his treatment of his fellows.

The idea of culture which came into being in the course of the last century and the revival of religion in the upper middle classes after the French revolution are to be accounted for by the necessity of obscuring this conflict between an ideology of freedom and a practice of oppression.

Both religion and culture offer salvation to the individual; while, since the industrial revolution, all our problems have been social. Religion and culture answer questions from groups as though they were being asked by individuals. The bourgeois, by feigning, with the help of his political ideology, to recognize in the half-starved factory hand a free individual, succeeded at once in constituting himself as a member of an aristocracy of merit (which culture made hereditary) and the worker as a being responsible for his own misfortunes. By looking upon the worker as an individual in theory, the employer could consider him as having sinned or as being closed to the 'higher values', or both, and could consequently make use of him as an anonymous unit. The grosser forms of capitalist oppression have, to be sure, disappeared in America and most of western Europe, but the habit of approaching social problems through the individual has taken root, and it is this that causes us to suppose that freedom (of concern to the individual) can have any meaning in countries where hunger (a social problem) is endemic. The function of culture was to confer upon the bourgeois the right to rule by virtue of his concern for 'civilization', and if the universities have been totally unsuccessful in spreading culture to the masses it is because they are proffering a commodity which the masses *do not need*, since their right to rule, by the bourgeois' own admission, requires no justification. Since, therefore, their position is not a usurped one, it should be possible for the masses to return to culture as an activity, and if this has not happened, I am convinced it is because the intelligentsia persist in regarding culture as a possession, as a means of artificially reproducing the 'divine' individual who passed away in 1789. 'Culture' of this kind is of no use to the unfortunate arts student who will be called upon to make a living; who is therefore primarily the member of a given group, and not primarily an individual concerned to acquire the right to occupy a privileged position and to

72

give quality or tension to a life of leisure. In other words, culture as commonly understood in the universities, instead of helping people to a sharper consciousness of themselves as function rather than as 'object', does its best to persuade them that there is no good life apart from opposition to the mass. We do not influence the course of events by criticizing them (as the young hegelians thought) but by joining forces with them (as Marx knew). Ortega y Gasset's 'modern barbarian' is a product of the universities, but the reorganization of curricula so as to ensure that the literary historian will have an understanding of the quantum theory and the scientist an appreciation of John Donne will alter nothing, because this would still be culture as possession; a culture which would sacrifice the group to the individual, just as the scientific approach (through psychology), which we discussed a moment ago, sacrifices the individual to the group. We need an entirely new departure before the spread of middle-class values (of which culture in the orthodox sense is one) has doped us into a final sleep.

Nietzsche is the supreme expression of the bourgeois' longing to change usurpation into divine right. The misery of the masses was a constant reproach since it could no longer be considered to be in the nature of things, and for those unwilling to protect themselves from it by hypocrisy the only alternative was to turn upon the masses and enslave or destroy them, thus founding a new aristocracy of divine individuals. Such is fascism—the apotheosis of the individual, while communism is the apotheosis of historical law which, in the case of the Russians, was temporarily incarnated in the person of Stalin.

But for the professional thinkers, the monks, there was no problem. Reason had triumphed and their task had become simply to prevent, through objectivity, any recrudescence of obscurantism. They continued to assume, as had the eighteenth century, that practice automatically adjusts itself to theory, and although our history for the past one hundred and fifty years is a long demonstration to the contrary, the monk still believes, or acts as though he still believes, that existence can safely be left to catch up with thought as best it may. The solution of the messiah was to turn the theory into certitude. But, in many cases, this came to be simply another form of the perpetual sacrifice of existence to essence; for the constant reworking of theory in the light of fact, which is characteristic of Marx, too often became in his followers the simple interpretation of the Word.

The picaresque novelist does no more than tell a story because life is what it always was and always will be; there is no enquiry, no outrage, the only question is, what is going to happen? Enquiry is still in the hands of the philosophers, and if their questions sometimes take the form of a *conte philosophique* it is because they have begun to think that life, as well as matter, may be fundamentally rational. But life remains, none the less, a derivative, and the French revolution was a shattering event not only socially and politically but metaphysically, because it indicated that life was not a by-product of thought, that it had a kind of independence and that, consequently, it might be profitable to mould thought upon life rather than the reverse. This was the work of Hegel and Marx, but whether you begin with the Idea or 'turn Hegel upside down' and begin with matter, the Real is still rational, and neither the monk nor the messiah start with history and human existence, their point of departure is the presupposition of rationality which will make it impossible, at least for all but the most honest of thinkers, to see life as it is in all its ambiguity. And yet life, rational or not, had now to be taken into account. Revolutionary ideology had conferred upon *all* men the status of human beings, who therefore came to form part of that Reality which it is the business of the artist to see and to see whole. But for what was perhaps the first time, at least on such a scale, reality and theory were in irreconcilable conflict.[1] In the past, thought had always been an explanation, never a plan of campaign; revolutions had been mere revolts, acts of desperation, not enterprises with the purpose of permanently altering the social order. The revolution had taught that something could be done about existence, and henceforth no artist of any integrity could depict it, there where it involved suffering, in a way which would not imply condemnation—to name was to denounce. One has only to compare Daumier to Chardin or Hogarth, the whole nineteenth-century tradition of realism to that of the preceding century. The rich vein of sentimentality which so curiously runs through the Enlightenment is the expression of an awareness of human suffering along with the conviction of its inevitability. We must not forget that initially the French revolution simply happened, it was not intended, and this is what distinguishes it most radically from the Russian and Chinese revolutions of the twentieth century. If senti-

[1] It is Dostoievski who gives the sharpest expression to this conflict when he says that an eternity of paradise could not make up for the suffering of a child.

mentality disappears in a Balzac or a Zola, it is because they hoped to be making a 'scientific' contribution toward a solution; and where that hope fades, as in Flaubert, Maupassant, Hardy, etc., its place is taken by a bitterness unthinkable in a society where practice is explained and justified by thought rather than being in violent conflict with it. Leibnitz explained how what was, had to be; and this was the basis of eighteenth-century optimism, which, despite *Candide*, was characteristic to some extent of Voltaire himself. In *l'Esprit des Lois*, Montesquieux writes almost exclusively of what is, not of what ought to be (except in so far as what ought to be was simply a clearer manifestation of the great rational Plan). In the following century, by contrast, when Hegel tried to halt the movement of his dialectic with christianity and the Prussian state, when, in other words, he began to talk in terms of what was rather than of what should be, he provoked the revolt of the young hegelians.

In his poem on the Lisbon earthquake, Voltaire wrote: 'One day all will be well, such is our hope.' All would be well when the ideas of the Enlightenment triumphed. With the revolution they did triumph, but what was to have been a universal liberation turned out to have been the liberation of a specific class only, a class which had come to power under false pretences and which, if it were to continue to govern without cynicism, would have to resort to hypocrisy. The nineteenth century, as Stendhal remarked, is that of hypocrisy. It is because the rule of the bourgeoisie was founded upon a lie that the position of the artist becomes delicate as it had never been; for where is he to look for Reality? In fact or in theory? He must choose because they are mutually exclusive; if he choses fact his work becomes a denunciation of which Picasso's *Le Repas Frugal* is the model, if he chooses theory he becomes responsible for the atrocities of Victorian art, its literature for virgins, so remote from fact that an attempt to return to it takes the form of futile revolt as in Hardy and D. H. Lawrence, or elegant disillusionment in the case of those who care less. British 'stupidity' is not of long standing, it came in with the industrial revolution. In preceding centuries, Britain had furnished the world with her full share of literary and philosophical geniuses and if, during the nineteenth century, she begins to provide almost exclusively for home consumption, it is because industrial greatness had a reverse which could not and yet had to be ignored. British 'stupidity' is simply the carefully nurtured ability to refuse existence to what actually is or happens.[1] There is no realist tradition of any importance in British literature and art after the eighteenth century because realism could no longer be simply a mirror held up to life, it was at the same time, and necessarily, a criticism and a protest.

The novelist, like all artists, must copy nature as his particular culture sees it, but the general theoretical acceptance of eighteenth-century ideology meant that the nineteenth-century novelist could not represent reality without simultaneously passing a judgement. This was, and remains, the dilemma of the novelist—to reconcile in himself the polemicist and the artist. Success is rare because the extremes of intelligence and love are destructive of one another; love (as in Balzac, Dickens) is indiscriminate, intelligence (as in Flaubert, Proust, Gide, Mann) is too exclusive. But these novelists, relatively speaking, have created work of a high order; in others, intelligence becomes mere adherence to a creed, in which case we have the thesis novel or even worse, social realism; or on the other hand, love becomes 'culture' or sentimentality to give the chatty insignificance of the bourgeois novel. Once again the messiah and the monk rub elbows, the art of each is equally far removed from reality whose place has been filled by an Absolute—a named and fixed principle for the messiah, for the deistic monk that hidden rationality which enables him without a qualm to turn thought into a game.

Art for art's sake turns an evasion into an ideal. It is a device which enables the artist to deal with reality without becoming a redresser of wrongs, he can at the same time contemplate the truth and ignore it—the supreme accomplishment of the nineteenth-century bourgeoisie. We hate the people we have grievously wronged, and the hatred of the bourgeoisie for the unwashed lower orders upon which, unfortunately, it depended, is curiously echoed in art which, from the mid-century onward, is characterized by a fascination for and at the same time an attempt to escape from the real. This often occurs within the same man, conspicuously in Flaubert, Baudelaire and Eliot, but also in Zola (toward the end of his career), in Huysmans, the Goncourts, George Moore. In Joyce and Proust, the phenomenon occurs not only in the same man but in the same book; the real is present in *Ulysses* and in *A la recherche du temps perdu*

[1] In this connection, one immediately thinks of the success the British middle classes have had in suppressing sex. It is also worth remarking that since the best cinema for the past two decades or so has been realist in inspiration, the British industry falls far behind the French, Italian and even the American. It is a matter of common knowledge that continental films are in 'bad taste'.

(both authors were scrupulous about verifying detail, however trivial), but only by reflection in a stream of consciousness or in the mirrored recesses of the Proustian *moi. Fin de siècle* aestheticism implied a strong sense of the increasing ugliness of the real along with a total impotence to do anything about it except, like Des Esseints, to sleep by day and shut oneself up by night or, like Ruskin, to convince the industrialists that beauty is greater than gain or, like Eliot, to make religion fit for consumption by the truly cultivated.[1]

The idea of culture as possession is inseparable from that of a roomy and sumptuously furnished Self. The 'objective interiority' which the renaissance inaugurates—conscience for the protestant, mind for the philosopher, honour for the nobleman—becomes, with romanticism, a perfumed if sometimes sinister labyrinth where Proust will discover the marvels of 'involuntary memory' and where Freud will come to grips with the minotaur. Private journals proliferate and literature becomes a kind of spelaeology, with writers descending into the self in search of 'originality', until Sartre, deciding that the self was not a domain but a 'stinking brine', kicked it over in *Being and Nothingness*. There were diaries before the nineteenth century, but Retz, Saint-Simon, Pepys, simply kept records of what happened, as did Boswell except for an occasional self-exhortation to greater *retenue*. After the revolution, however, for the diarist as for the novelist, it is impossible simply to take note of an event or person without simultaneously declaring a partisanship;[2] that is, without simultaneously identifying oneself. Our attempts to get at the nature of the exterior world are at the same time efforts toward self-identification; to each historical world view corresponds a different conception of man. Before the nineteenth century, objects, but above all other men, mirrored identities with infallible accuracy, a man was precisely what his accent and his clothing announced. After the turn of the century, however, both the pomp of the aristocrat and the misery of the worker or peasant were mere appearances,

[1] In his *Journal des Faux-Monnayeurs* Gide, though referring to the symbolist poets, characterizes the entire literature of the period: 'Poetry became a refuge for them; the only escape from a hideous reality; they plunged themselves into it with the ardour of despair.'

[2] Events had come to require an interpretation, and the fact that Flaubert tries to refuse one to the events of 1848 in *l'Education Sentimentale* is one of the reasons for the mausoleum-like atmosphere of the novel which makes it a favourite with academics. It is a novel which demonstrates that there is nothing to be done.

the 'inner world' became the only unattackable guarantee of mission or distinction. The romantic is primarily one who tries to interpret the world with reference to the self rather than the self with reference to the world, and while nature can be made in some degree to reflect the self, other men cannot, so the life of the romantic is one of lonely frustration. Maine de Biran is the nineteenth-century's Saint-Simon, but instead of a picture of the court of Louis XVIII we have one of Maine de Biran himself; not from the 'outside' in the fashion of Montaigne, nor is it a question of motivation or self-justification as in Rousseau, it is a long tireless and neurotically anxious act of self-examination. The difference is not one of personalities, for if Maine de Biran had had the assurance of a Saint-Simon he would have been ridiculous. We remarked that conscience came into being when God ceased to be visible; somewhat the same process occurs with the self when the exterior world ceases to make sense or when it becomes an unpleasant place in which to live. The monarchy was a sham, and the condition of the people flagrantly contradicted middle-class talk of progress as well as its revolutionary principles. Maine de Biran is a figure of great historical interest because instead of using the self as a refuge like the romantics, as an objective interiority like the idealists and like Proust, or as an excuse like the bourgeois individual, he looks upon it as did Kierkegaard as the source of truth. Thus he speaks of a *sens intime*, or a *sens intérieur*, of which logic and reason would be simply the tools. When he writes: 'I deny that we can be deceived by a feeling of evidence', he anticipates in part Husserl's intentionality and Sartre's *cogito préréflexif*. But Maine de Biran was also very much of his own time, and as his life wore on he came more and more to look upon this *sens intime* as a means of getting in touch with God. However, if we are going to argue that truth is accessible to consciousness, then we can no longer regard it as single and absolute, it must vary from one part of the earth to another, and from one age to another. We have seen one aspect of this reduction of truth to appearance in cubism. If we can find something similar in literature, we shall no doubt learn how all this affects the inner as well as the outer world.

The star of Maine de Biran's great contemporary, Stendhal, continues to rise and now outshines that of all other nineteenth-century French novelists. Balzac, Flaubert and even Proust have become classics, in my meaning of the word; they have been largely 'absorbed', while Stendhal still resists. We must try to find out why.

I have argued that what we must bear constantly in mind in thinking about the nineteenth century is the conflict between existence and theory inaugurated by the *theoretical* triumph of revolutionary ideology. There could only be one solution apart from a greater or lesser degree of hypocrisy—the solution of Maine de Biran, that of making the truth reside in existence rather than in theory. Everyone remarks the 'contradiction' between Marx's Jovian indignations and his talk of economic or historical law, between his subjective reactions (his existence) and theory. But here is precisely the difference between intelligence and genius, here is why 'great thoughts come from the heart'. To the furnishing of explanations or the construction of theories, great intelligence suffices, but to cause these theories to grow out of the 'subjective' needs and aspirations of men, to make them into instruments of human endeavour so effective that they become 'objective law', this is the work of genius. The nineteenth century was full of intelligent 'law makers', but their thinking grew almost exclusively out of other thoughts, while the thought of Marx grew like a tree out of the soil of immediate problems of human welfare which it is always tempting to ignore because they introduce such hellish complications. The source of the wealth of nations, according to Marx, is unpaid labour. We are dealing here as much with a created truth as with a discovered law, a lever with which to move the earth, and things will begin to go wrong because Marx's disciples imagined that they had been equipped with a 'law' rather than with a tool. Error crept in in proportion as marxism became an entirely objective discipline, in proportion as it substituted a historical determination for historical possibilities and perspectives inspired, as in Marx, by a *subjective* experience of human needs. It has become the rather silly practice to attempt to discredit Marx by pointing out that a number of his prophecies have not been realized. But they could only have been realized if nineteenth-century scientism had been a sound philosophy, and we have presumably left scientism far behind. In other words, Marx is most commonly criticized for not having performed the impossible.

Hypocrisy is simply the denial of some subjective evidence. It occurs not only in the bourgeois who denies that his conduct is in conflict with his political and religious ideology, but also in the revolutionary who denies that a crime is a crime if committed for exalted motives. The whole import of the work of Dostoievski is to expose this hypocrisy, to argue that we must be guided by our sub-

79

jective abhorrence of crime rather than by the objective justifications that intelligence can readily provide. Raskolnikov, like all of Dostoievski's characters who go wrong (even to some of those in the short stories, like the hero of *An Unfortunate Incident*) is misled by his reason, which he allows to override the objections of subjectivity. But to some extent, Dostoievski's *sens intérieur* is not to be distinguished from the infallible conscience of religious thinking, and in this respect he was wrong because conscience is passive. Dostoievski was telling his compatriots what not to do in a country where everything remained to be done.

We have reached the point where it is easy for us to recognize in Stendhal what it was that caused him to be to such an extraordinary extent ahead of his time. The heroes of Stendhal do not advance in knowledge of the world, it is they themselves who are the source of truth, and society destroys them for their presumption. Stendhal sits in judgement upon the world, and he judges in his own name. It is in this way that Maine de Biran's *sens intime* finds its true employment; for we have the choice of considering truth to be hidden, in which case it is natural to posit an active faculty (reason) designed to ferret it out; or, if we are going to make truth accessible to subjective feeling, then it must, at the same time, be regarded as *evident*, otherwise we fall into irrationality which consists, as we have seen, not in having recourse to 'subjectivity', but, on the contrary, in being over precise about the nature of the hidden Absolute. The truth that Stendhal the 'egoist' encounters in himself is that of all men, obscured in some by hypocrisy, in others by faith in more sensational answers.

The evidence of social and moral truths is the equivalent in another domain of the reality painted by the modern artist, a reality which is visual, not mental, and in this sense evident. Just as the new vision of a Picasso is closed to many of us because our perception is interfered with by what we have learned about the nature of objects, so our ability to respond to what a given situation evidently demands, is interfered with by what we have learned about morality. This is the source of Stendhal's 'immoralism' which intrigued Nietzsche and Gide. Morality as a code, applicable to all or most situations shields us from an arduous life as our 'scientific' perception shields us from the absurd. But it is always a mistake to give up fullness for correctness—there are no wise virgins.

The eighteenth century had a tendency to make man the measure, while retaining confidence in an intelligibility independent of him.

It is this contradiction that tormented the Promethean romantic, made possible the mystifications by which the bourgeoisie tried to legitimatize its domination, and gave birth, in the name of man himself this time, to new fanaticisms. Stendhal is the supreme product of the Enlightenment because he alone mockingly refuses credence to caste and system, his one centre of reference being what all men know indubitably on those rare occasions when they consent to stop playing a role.

Stendhal was a child of the revolution. He knew that the old legitimacy had gone and that what had taken its place was a mere façade. The only real legitimacy would have to be one of merit. But while in the past merit could be tolerated or even encouraged because it did not threaten the social order (opposition to the *philosophes* came for the most part from the Church), the new ruling class had to close their ranks against it while feigning to keep them open. This, as we have already seen, is one of the functions of culture which is at once an activity (merit) and a divine right (privilege).[1] 'Man is a sorcerer for man', someone has remarked, but no man is a sorcerer for himself, and from the rituals of the medicine men to the displays of the wealthy, the purpose is to proclaim an inherent endowment for which there is *no subjective evidence whatever*. Yet the sorcerer is not entirely a hypocrite; the very fact that subjectively we are not thing, but only ceaseless movement, makes it natural, almost inevitable, to try to define ourselves from without by ceremony and possession. But however natural it may be to feel our self-esteem reassured by, for example, robes of office, we remain vulnerable to the first sardonic glance, to the first person who refuses to be taken in, the first person who, giving to a subjective evidence an objective validity, views us as we view ourselves. This is the view which Stendhal takes of restoration society, so desperately busy re-establishing appearances to shield from itself the absence of the old realities; it is today the view that Sartre takes of the *salauds*, a view at once unanswerable and easily reasoned away. We know that pomp and circumstance (including the academic) would mirror an inner essence that is not really there—but prove it. Solipsism is high philosophical comedy. The sweet sorrow of such isolation—it would have had to be invented.

[1] The *académie française* (from which real merit is very frequently excluded) and the English public schools (where merit is encouraged to become physical or moral rather than intellectual) are typical institutions concerned with the preservation of occidental culture.

As late as Proust and Freud (or, for that matter, Husserl himself, in his later work), men were trying to reconstitute a self that Stendhal had long since begun to suppress. We have only to compare his heroes to those of Balzac (or Dickens) to be aware how little Stendhal was of his own time. We are rarely unable to place a label upon Balzac's characters, we are still in the ancient world of types come down to us from Theophrastus; Balzac simply added a fat supplement to bring Molière and La Bruyère up to date. There are species of men as there are species of plants and animals, and to describe his environment is to describe the man himself. The shape of a nose or chin in the novels of Balzac reveals a person's nature as unmistakably as its colour and size identifies a bird. If men are of the nature of things, furthermore, then they may be arranged in a hierarchy, ascending from Vautrin with hell-fire licking at his heels to Seraphita about to pass over into angelhood. There is therefore an Order that no revolution can ever shake, and Balzac is full of sorcerers who embody aspects of that Order, with Vautrin himself as much a part of it as the Devil is a part of the christian Order. Vautrin's judgement upon society is invalid because he *had* to make it, it was in his 'nature' to do so; and that his criminality should have been a reasoned one illustrates that much more forcibly (as in the case of Dostoievski) the necessity of adhering to the comfortable old hierarchies, political (Balzac was a royalist) or spiritual, however unsatisfactory from a purely rational point of view they may be.

No character of Balzac can act in such a way as to belie his nature, because his acts are a simple manifestation. With Stendhal, on the contrary, acts do not manifest a nature, they *constitute* it. Julien Sorel knows that he will never be any more than what he does, hence the constant self-discipline with the aid of which he literally creates himself. The *parvenu* (a familiar figure in Balzac) does not menace the social order, he reinforces it; not only because he is prepared to humiliate himself for its sake, but because being of the wrong species, like the *bourgeois gentilhomme*, he can never completely succeed. But a Julien Sorel or a Lucien Leuwen do not succeed, not because they are unable to, but because to occupy an exalted place in the social order is to exchange what is most precious in man, his indetermination, for the acceptance of a role. The nauseating insipidity of public declarations derives from the fact that the official concerned speaks as a Member of Parliament, as a professor, as an executive, never as a mere man. He sacrifices what he ought to say as a man to what, with a greater or lesser degree of hypocrisy, he takes it upon himself to say as an objective identity. The heroes of Stendhal refuse an identity; we remember them for what they did, not for what they were, and we do not see their like again until Malraux and Hemingway. Love, for Stendhal, is important not for how it makes people feel, but for what it causes them to do; not because it bestows an identity, but because it destroys one—Madame de Rênal ceases to be a wife and mother, Mademoiselle de Chasteller an aristocrat, Julien Sorel a plebeian, etc. Of all Stendhal creatures, Fabrice of *La Chartreuse de Parme* is perhaps the 'purest', precisely because, divorced from his acts, there remains even less of him than of the others. He is all 'exteriority', entirely absorbed by doing, completely unconcerned about being.[1]

The lesson of Stendhal is that a man does not have a fixed identity, and that most of our ills, social as well as individual, issue from the detestable habit of feigning one. The purpose of an identity, or objective self, whether it be that of the perfect gentleman whose every movement is regulated by current usage, or that of the Nazi Aryan, is not to oppose but to conform. This is clearly not the intent of people who talk of an 'opposing self', or, like the personalists, of the rights of the person or individual; but is not the 'opposing self' quite simply the 'subjective' equivalent of that objective principle which the western intellectual assumes to be there but which he declines to name? The only difference between the political or religious militant and the cultivated 'opposing' intellectual is that the two former name their absolute while the latter does not. And if the intellectual denies faith in some supreme principle working for good, then his opposition, being that of the self and therefore politically ineffectual, is little less than criminal. The individual, which it has

---

[1] I am giving this attention to Stendhal because the modern novel stems from him as poetry does from Baudelaire and painting from Cézanne. The novel since Joyce and Proust marks a progressive dissolution of the self (conspicuously of course in the American novel). Julien Sorel, and the Meursault of Camus's *l'Etranger* were executed for what was, fundamentally, the same crime—the refusal to feign an identity which society sought to impose but which subjectivity could not confirm. Julien affronted society by demonstrating that one was not by essence a peasant, and Meursault by refusing to pretend that he entertained feelings which are alleged to belong *essentially* to 'human nature'. Two of France's most remarkable present-day novelists, Natalie Sarraute and Alain Robbe-Grillet, even though they take opposing views of their craft, both produce books in which the self has quite vanished; M. Robbe-Grillet ignores it by principle, and Natalie Sarraute's analyses fail to disclose one.

become the mission of the intellectuals to defend, is as elusive as the non-existent objective point of view which our thinkers all adopt. We may be sure, however, that it is not the individual as such, the individual simply as a human being, which is meant here, for that leads to the 'subjective' anarchy of disrespect characteristic of the heroes of Stendhal or, worse still, to the perpetual discontent of the worker who places his own well-being above 'that of the nation'. What is meant is the individual who has achieved such a degree of cultural enrichment or psychological complexity that he is no longer able to accept the attitudes and opinions of the mass of the population. He therefore goes into opposition in the name of a cultural heritage menaced not only by indifference but by continual attempts at partisan exploitation.

The question here is, are the values of the 'opposing self', that is of culture as a possession, a valid ideal for all men? Employers speak of increases in wages as not being in the 'interests of the nation', and I have the impression that the academic intellectual's defence of culture is at the same time very much a defence of himself. Is it altogether by accident that an institution like the Third Programme, with its minute listening audience, should have become established in a country which has resisted more successfully than any other the breaking up of its social strata? The imperturbable self-confidence of the British intellectual may account in part for his readiness to reveal in these broadcasts all the pompous vacuity of culture as possession. The flash of indignation, an impatient irreverence, or merely some earthy humour that would have come from the *man*, never pierces the veneer of the scholar and gentleman; the man, with his rich fund of subjective truths, the truths he feels because they are evident and awaiting expression, never succeeds in making himself heard above the somnolent murmur of the objective automaton.

The academic who 'universalizes' his particular and peculiar way of life is being as naïve as the christian who considers his religion truer than the others. The academics and the intellectuals in general have a job to perform. Their position is a privileged one because of the importance of the job and not because they lead, thanks to their culture, a fuller life and are the depositories of a heritage which everyone should aspire to share. Culture as possession does not make a better individual; it makes a different one; and one who, still accepting the scientific but none the less arbitrary separation of the physical from the mental, has made the latter realm his own. The truth, for these individuals, is the end product of a mental process objectively conducted; their 'opposition' is consequently always passive and futile, and in addition, they know it to be such, since whatever one thinks of Marx, it is impossible to go back to a stage of our civilization where thought could serenely evolve in total independence of the brutal realities of existence.

The two objectivities of the classical scientific world view, that of a truth independent of time and place and that of a mental apparatus capable of knowing it, involve, as we have seen, truths or entities that are hidden. For the past century or so, there has been a growing tendency in occidental culture to refuse credence to the hidden, and while this is clear enough in phenomenology and existentialism, it also appears to me the best approach to a fuller understanding of modern art and literature. The cubists depict the world as it appears (or, sometimes, which comes to the same thing, they create objects which are not in nature), not the well-ordered static world which we unconsciously construct and which is more a product of the mind than of the senses. Stendhal, who was even more in advance of his time than he thought, begins the suppression of 'interiority'.

The world of the cubists, of modern poetry, of Kafka, Michaux, Beckett, etc., is an absurd one. But unless we are of those who pursue, anachronistically, the search for complete intelligibility, its absurdity is not entire. Cubism does not only make sense aesthetically, it reveals long-neglected aspects of the real, and *The Castle* conveys a meaning. It is a meaning, however, which is never explicit, it is one which must, in large measure, come from the reader,[1] and this is precisely the situation obtaining between the world and man. What meaning there is in the world is one which we in part put there; but not, of course, as Kant supposed this process to take place. We have eliminated the 'inner world', and knowledge, therefore, is the constitution of a partial meaning in accordance with our needs, and not the discovery of a total meaning with the assistance of some inner apparatus. Knowledge is not a distillation of the mind, it is an act in the sense of intention or choice.

We shall have to develop these ideas somewhat; they may help us to decide what the job of the intellectual really is. There is no task more urgent.

[1] Valéry said that his poetry had the meaning the reader wished to give it.

85

III

PHILOSOPHERS often like to think of themselves as being men who see difficulties in what appears perfectly clear to others. Like Socrates, they are questioners. But their difficulties are of a peculiar kind—no one suffers for having been unaware of them. The mechanic who overlooks a difficulty which some repair is going to involve, risks causing himself much unnecessary work, and there is no danger that he will not sooner or later encounter the difficulty. One does not encounter the philosopher's difficulty, however (which, when sufficiently grave is called a 'problem of philosophy'), without considerable effort; it must be patiently pointed out to us and even then we do not always see it.

It is for this reason that our professional questioners[1] never ask embarrassing questions as even children sometimes do. An embarrassing question arises when a man (frequently 'ill-bred' or 'ill-educated') insists upon ignoring an objective 'explanation' in order to identify a subjective intention; that is, he ignores the 'difficulty' of determining an unseen 'cause', preoccupied as he is to reacting to an evidence. For example, the adolescent fortunate enough to be able to give free reign to his sexual appetites is reacting to an evidence which society, out of a mixture of gratuitous cruelty and cowardice, does its best to obscure. Or again, the survival of strong class feeling in Britain is a legitimate source of wonder and dismay.

[1] Which is to say, our intellectuals almost as a whole, since between fanaticism and anarchical question asking, they see no middle course.

The 'explanations' of the historian or sociologist cause us to slight the fact (which is the first to strike the ignorant) that someone is responsible for the continued existence of this absurd mentality, it is willed, it has a significance, otherwise it would have disappeared. But if things are as they are mainly because certain people want them to be that way, what becomes of the intellectual whose business it is to understand and explain?

The idea of responsibility, however, is by no means unknown to the objective society, but it is applied to our enemies, never to ourselves. The communists, for example, were responsible for the creation of an oppressive police state in Russia; the very weighty historical circumstances which help to explain this development are seldom dwelt upon.[1] On the other hand, the responsibility for the Kenya 'detention' camps, the situation in Cyprus, the Suez war which helped decide the Russians to intervene in Hungary and which could have led to a world war, is not ours. The unspeakable degradation in which the masses of the people living in Egypt and the near east pass their lives is the result of well-known historical 'causes'; no one is responsible for it, least of all us. The oil industry is regulated by economic 'law', not by men. The communists are responsible for the silliness of social realism in art and literature; no one is responsible for the sustained imbecility of our press, nor for the present spiritual vacuum in Anglo-Saxon countries, least of all the academics. It is vital for us to look for responsibilities behind the evil of communism, otherwise we shall find obvious explanations for it—the dead hand of marxist scientism, the almost medieval backwardness of the Russian people in 1917, etc. For our particular evil, however, there is only one explanation—self-interest; we therefore concentrate our attention not upon responsibility (that would be a superficial view) but upon hard historical fact and economic law.

I can understand the irritation of the reader who, expecting a dispassionate development of idea, is continually stumbling over these nastily aggressive passages. But, provided it is selfless, the best part of a man is his indignation. It is good that people should detest the Russian intervention in Hungary, that the flimsy fiction of objectivity in the academic should be dropped; what is distressing is that this indignation should be so often limited to communist misdeeds,

[1] For example, the necessity of developing heavy industry which involved forcing people into the cities, and then of forcing the peasants to produce more in order to feed the greatly augmented urban population.

that it should stop short at Spain and Portugal, for example, at Kenya, South Africa, Guatemala, British New Guinea, Algeria, etc. I admit, of course, that slow starvation makes less noise than Russian tanks.

We are careful how we bestow our indignation because an emotion is, in the final analysis, a kind of intention; it is not something that happens to us, it is something we do.[1] An event does not provoke an emotional reaction in us, it is our reaction that constitutes the nature of the event. By way of a simple illustration of what is meant here: we often say things to others which will admit of several interpretations, and not infrequently we will accept whatever meaning they fix upon—their reaction will constitute the remark as one made in fun or as an insult. Thus words which, in themselves, 'objectively', were little more than an emission of breath have bestowed upon them by a subjective reaction an objective existence which we may well assume and which could have an important influence upon our life. Or again, on a different level, the Soviet repression of the Hungarian revolt was not *in itself* an inexcusable barbarism, it was constituted as such by our reaction to it. Had this event taken place sometime before the nineteenth century when the sacking of towns with all that went with it was a more or less accepted procedure, the Russians would have been extolled for their restraint.

It must not be supposed that subjectivity (and here the reader will recall the way in which this term was defined in the introduction) is constitutive only of meaning or significance. It goes further than that.

Empiricism begins with a 'pre-fabricated' world which had been waiting until approximately the fifteenth century for men to begin in earnest to take its measurements and sound its depths. This is a world which is 'already there'; and it is still difficult to convince the empiricist that he does not start from the beginning at all, he starts with an assumption, and one which, whether he likes it or not, is metaphysical. He assumes a ready-made world full of labeled objects, and the logician persists in supposing that to manipulate the labels is to manipulate the objects. But although the labels make up a more or less coherent structure, it is one which, taken as a whole, is arbitrary; and the significance of cubism is to show that the empirico-

[1] Although, to be sure, a given type of emotional reaction (a sharp temper, etc.) may become so habitual that we are, in part at least, its victims.

88

rationalist structure is not obligatory[1] (in the sense of being all-inclusive) because to name is not to identify but, in part, to constitute. Cubism refuses to constitute the stretch of lawn as such. A photograph is not in the first instance the picture of a friend, it is a piece of paper with patches of black and white upon it. Our recognition of the subject is therefore a constitutive act, and if we let the photograph be the exterior world, then one aspect of cubism is the representation of the black and white patches in an aesthetically pleasing manner.

Let us express all this now in a somewhat different way. There is a 'problem' of perception only if we accept post-medieval metaphysics, according to which the Real is independent of the processes by which we take cognizance of it. The problem now, and it has proven to be insoluble, is to explain how the mental communicates with the physical. The temptation is to eliminate one of the terms. But if everything (or the essential) is mental, then we cannot account for error; if everything is physical, then we cannot account for significance. With the idealists we know far less than we should; with the empiricists, a great deal more.

If, in considering perception, we eliminate the whole traditional construction—primary and secondary qualities, sense data, association of ideas, etc., etc.—precisely because it is a construction and not an experience, then we are left with two basic facts which logically exclude one another but which are none the less indubitable. First, we perceive objects necessarily in a given perspective, i.e. an object is never seen to be what it is known to be; a cube, for example, from whatever angle we view it looks like anything but a cube; and yet, secondly, we instantly recognize it as a cube. Empirical explanations will not do because it is impossible to see how even an unlimited number of perspectives could add up to a cube without already being related in some way to one another, i.e. without already being views of a cube.[2] Intellectualism, on the other hand,

[1] In literature, this occurs most deliberately and competently in Sartre's *La Nausée*, which is not philosophical literature, but literature which makes a contribution to philosophy. It marks the full flowering of that principle we found to constitute the originality of Stendhal—the only objective truth which is not illusory is attained through subjectivity. In the case of the hero of Sartre's novel, a feeling of 'nausea' leads to a number of discoveries about the nature of the world and of man.

[2] Experiment has failed to give any support to theories of 'brain traces'. For a fuller development of the present argument, see Merleau-Ponty, *La Structure du Comportement* (Presses Universitaires, 1953, p. 202), and Husserl's *Cartesian Meditations*, II, 17–18.

posits the existence of the cube independently of its successive appearances; but in so doing it renders superfluous the functioning of the judgement which is supposed to explain the independent existence of the cube.

If we are going to overcome these difficulties without shirking the fundamental contradiction of perception which I have just mentioned, then we must call into question the hidden postulate of all of classical epistemology—the supposition that the world *precedes* our consciousness of it, that the problem of how we know may be reduced to the problem of how we identify. If we do this, we can accept uncompromisingly the insuperable 'perspectivism' of perception and yet at the same time explain recognition, since we are free now to see in consciousness a constitutive act.[1] Furthermore, the very fact that perception is circumscribed by a given perspective guarantees the constitution of an objective world, since the exigencies of historical time and place are the same for all.[2]

I think the best way to understand what has been called the copernican revolution of modern thought (and it is certainly all of that) is to envisage it in the way just suggested: it amounts primarily to giving up all attempts to evade the fact that man is *situated*, that he is confined to a given historical and physical perspective. It amounts, in other words, to renouncing total intelligibility through intellection in exchange for partial truths which offer the advantage of being subjectively evident for the simple reason that we ourselves have constituted them. It amounts, ultimately, though none of the phenomenologists, and of the existentialists only Sartre has gone this far, it amounts ultimately to the substitution of act (in the sense of conduct) for contemplation. Classical objectivity which is essentially the refusal to accept the ineluctable limitations of perspective is also a choice enabling the monk to decline the responsibilities of participation and (which comes to the same thing) enabling the messiah to act independently of the special requirements of a particular situation.

[1] When cubism depicts a recognizable object, it often does so in attempting to present it 'all at once'; it telescopes a sequence of perspectives into simultaneity, and so expresses the truth that we actually see the entire object even though only a single aspect of it is visible at one time. A perceived object is both physical and mental, an 'objective constitution'.

[2] For example, two workmen recognize the same tool in a given object because, in a wider perspective than that of simple perception, they are *both* engaged in an undertaking which would be impossible without the objective constitution of the object as the appropriate tool.

We saw that the 'geometrization' of the universe accomplished by renaissance science brought about the withdrawal of God to distances which made the sensory communication of the middle ages unacceptable, but which was no barrier to mind or conscience.[1] I think we may consider that the second copernican revolution completes the half-suppression of God effected by scientific thought. It introduces the first genuine atheism inasmuch as intelligibility is conceived as coming from man himself and not from some universal harmony of scientific necessity which is but another way in which to imagine God. The intellectuals are the priesthood of a vanished religion; and if this religion of 'reason', which surreptitiously posits an activity in what is known in order to countenance inactivity in the knower, lingers on like an embalmed corpse for as long as has the religion of revelation, the future holds little promise.

If it is true, as Eddington writes, that classical physics was rescued from a cul-de-sac by reconciling itself to the existence of a certain number of unknowables, then as might have been expected, the new philosophical world view would appear to have a profound analogy not only with art but also with science. Relativity, the quantum theory and phenomenology came into being within a very few years of each other, and in each case, a non-existent everything is given up in order to obtain a tangible more; in each case 'blanket' concepts are declared to be covering far less than had been hoped. These thinkers and scientists have divided the universe into 'structures', each one of which has its own form of intelligibility (gravitation, for example, is a useful concept only when associated with a given structure). One wonders why science should have been exclusively a product of modern western European civilization; why did the Greeks stop short of it, why the Chinese? A good marxist could no doubt give some quite convincing answers, but surely christianity's long evolution toward an ever-stricter *monotheism* which culminates in the protestant suppression of the saints is not without significance here. Science, as we have seen, is an orientation, not a discovery; and its overriding purpose has always been to achieve absolute unity, to reduce many to one, to give a final solution, one is tempted to say, to the problem of the trinity. It is for this reason that Plato is the

[1] In his admirable book *Le Dieu Caché*, Lucien Goldmann finds in this simultaneous presence-absence of God the source of what he calls the 'tragic vision' (as opposed to the rationalist and dialectical) which he ascribes to Pascal, Racine and Kant.

father-thinker of our entire culture. Aristotle became known only toward the end of the middle ages. The spread of his philosophy caused the Church from time to time much misgiving, and the fact that it finally triumphed in Thomism was perhaps a tragedy for catholicism since it was unable to readjust itself to the enthusiastic return to Plato which came with the renaissance. We might describe the change which is coming over the way in which we think about the world as the giving up of this ancient 'unitarianism', of this 'monotheistic' craving for a single all-embracing principle. It is this principle, which would have made ours the point of view of God, that we have at last acknowledged to be unknowable. There is not, according to Einstein, a single universal time, but many. Causality, at least in its present form, is not of universal applicability judging from the comportment of atoms; and, in any case, according to Husserl, scientific truth, like all truth, is 'regional'. For classical epistemology an object is either known or not known, there is either truth or error; we see now that an object is both known and not known, because it can be perceived only in a given perspective. The problem of protestant theology was to reconcile natural law with divine omnipotence, and the purpose of predestination was to guarantee the prestige of God. Now the stakes have risen. There is the danger not only of a powerless deity, but of an ignorant one; for it is becoming just as difficult for us to conceive a God capable of assuming the 'exhaustive' point of view of the objective scholar as it once was for us to conceive a God who could suspend the functioning of natural law.

Books like Albert Camus's *l'Homme Révolté* and Karl Popper's *The Open Society and its Enemies* are saying what we in this part of the world are very happy to hear; namely, to quote Popper, 'history has no meaning'. In this way, marxism appears not only 'morally', but historically wrong; in this way, the monk vindicates his meditative aloofness or, in the case of Camus's book, the messiah admits he has been a fool—in the future, he will aim only at temporary alleviation when conditions become unendurable. The unanimity with which the intellectuals have overlooked what is constructive in contemporary thought was to be expected, for if we extend the notion of 'perspective' to history (following in this the precedent of classical epistemology whose 'unsituated' perception of objects was applied also to the study of history), not only does history have a

92

meaning, it is one for which we are responsible, one which we in some degree constitute. On the contrary, to say that history has no meaning is for the monk to preserve the barren all-embracing point of view of objectivity, and for the messiah to continue to act ineffectively; this time, not because act is related to principle rather than to need, but because it has no future. In brief, nothing has changed; except, of course, ideas; but it is not disagreeable to have new ideas provided that they remain ends in themselves. How, otherwise, is the scholar to protect himself from that exasperating sense of urgency which events of the day create in us and which is so prejudicial to the mental serenity indispensable to solid thinking?

To be sure, Popper repeatedly remarks that we are the makers of our fate, but it must not be supposed that he means 'make' in the sense of 'plan' or 'construct'. This work has already been done; the 'open society' already exists, it is ours and all we need do is protect it. Thus history culminates not in the dictatorship of the proletariat but, which is much more convenient, in the open society. The objective society has developed toward history and politics a maginot line mentality which invites disaster. It consists in mouthing such formulae as 'we must strengthen our democratic institutions', 'we must raise the standard of living in backward areas', etc. It is reassuring to think that this is precisely what we have been doing for the past century and a half, that history should be so static, that we should be able to confront the 'forces of evil' with so solid a rank of business men, missionaries and intellectuals all freely and spontaneously subscribing to the same slogans.

No one will quarrel with Popper's 'critical rationalism' except to say that it is irrelevant; for it consists in never forgetting that 'I may be right and you may be wrong'. But in matters of vital importance to all of us, we always know perfectly well who is right and who is wrong. One need only think of the history of fascism between the wars, of racism in South Africa and elsewhere, of the Suez war, of the 'question' of banning nuclear tests, etc. The objective intellectual will always take what the French call 'the point of view of Sirius'; and, of course, if one takes a sufficiently long view, what was at first clear becomes so infernally complex as to make all action appear inexcusably ill-considered.

Reason as speculation, as the attempt to decide who is right and who is wrong, is appropriate to the 'theological' civilization of the monk and the messiah. If, like Popper, and no doubt the majority of present-day intellectuals, we are to consider history as having no meaning, then it is not enough to conclude simply that right and wrong will be just that much more difficult to discern, that we must be that much more critical of dogmatism, that we must exercise that much more tolerance. By arguing in this way, the monk does no more than prolong his anachronistic quarrel with the messiah; he is trying to reconcile his long established abstentionism, or reason as speculation, with a world view which forces upon us a reassessment of the role of reason.

The monk accepts the suppression of meaning, yet retains reason considered primarily as an instrument for gaining access to meaning.

What this amounts to in practice is the reduction of reason to the status of pure criticism. This is why Anglo-Saxon society has at the moment no political or philosophical thought. Reason, as classical epistemology conceives it, requires a world view based upon the notion of pre-constituted meaning; take away the meaning and reason turns in a void. Reason cannot construct, it leads us to the already constructed. But if the world has no 'built in' rationality, we are cut off from our future, and all that remains is to issue pleas for more tolerance or, in hard times, endure the coming of the father figures. The objective society is trying to live in a twentieth-century world, an 'absurd' world, with a conception of reason which belongs to another age. The reason of the Enlightenment was critical also, almost exclusively so, but this did not amount to depriving men of a future precisely because the world *had* a meaning. Criticism was a constructive activity since religious and political intolerance alone prevented the emerging of an underlying rationality.

If philosophical, historical and political thought is to break out of the text-books, it must begin to elaborate a programme, it must stop its tireless waiting for the facts to organize themselves into a decipherable pattern which, in any case, the objective society would be the first to find inacceptable, just as the Church would know better than to believe that Christ had returned. The acquisitive and objective societies have grown old together in blissful wedlock. There is no reason to suppose that they will not be laid to rest together, inseparable in death as in life. But in the meantime, as is often the case with old people in positions of authority, they bar the way while serving no useful purpose. They deny us the right not only to build a better future, but even to plan one, even to suppose that one is possible.

94

Science and classical rationalism are interested only in what is clear, and they do not stop to enquire whether what is clear may always be equated with what is true or what is essential. The paradoxes of Zeno have been sitting like patience on the monuments of western philosophy. The only way we can think movement is to deny it—the only way we can be clear about life is to think it, but this can very easily bear no relation whatever to living it. Zeno's arrow stops for the philosopher who segments its trajectory, but not for the man who gets it in the neck. Where is the truth, in the philosopher's quandary or in the corpse? This, of course, is a modern question; one that must be asked because atomic bombs have replaced arrows. In Zeno's time, and until recently, the corpse made sense because warfare was one of the ways in which a man fulfilled himself. All wars were, in a sense, just wars. Our problem now is to bring the corpse to the philosopher's attention. He must be made to adapt his thought to the peculiar requirements of life as it is lived, and to stop suppressing existence for the sake of simplicity and clarity. One achieves clarity by a process of abstraction, by leaving out the 'accidental'; but the end product is not a more fundamental reality, it is a different kind of reality, and one, furthermore, which is not 'already there', but which we in part manufacture.

Orthodox thought replaces the real by the imaginary. Both Zeno's arrow and Galileo's projectile are imaginary because it is only by imagining it that an object may be made 'clear'; that is, may be divorced from the 'perspectivism' to which philosophy, up until Husserl, had been unable to reconcile itself. Galileo's imaginary projectile has changed the face of the world; but apart from science the supposition that the imaginary is the 'essence' of the real is what we call fanaticism. In the imaginary, we achieve full possession of the object; it is exhaustively known, precisely because it is non-existent because we have ceased to be situated in respect to it. The messiah can be certain because his Absolute is non-existent. But the monk is no less dogmatic—about the necessity of combating dogmatism, and his certitude also is based upon a miraculous liberation from perspective which he calls the objective point of view. Destalinization is simply the beginning of the end of the communists' blind faith in the imaginary laws of history, and the messiah has therefore begun to progress towards a healthy scepticism which, if the international situation permits, will eventually lead him back to reality. On the contrary, the western intellectual appears to me to be actually regressing. As

95

we have seen, the only justification for objectivity as practised by the monk is confidence in the existence of a rational principle which will inevitably prevent the utter and irretrievable dislocation of human life. If the existence of such a principle is called into doubt, as is now the case, then objectivity is an invitation to disaster. We said that eighteenth- and nineteenth-century thinkers assumed some kind of universal order while suppressing the divine mind from which alone it could have issued. The monk of today makes the reverse error, he postulates a mind with no order for it to think, or, which comes to the same thing, he accepts, while advocating a few minor adjustments, existing social arrangements as the best we can hope for. In fact, feeling the need to oppose something in the way of an ideology to communism,[1] and determined at the same time to preserve his imaginary objective point of view, the monk has had to freeze bourgeois government into a definitive historical acquisition called democratic pluralism. The 'fanatical opposition to fanaticism' amounts, therefore, in practice, to shoring up the existing order, to making of it that Absolute which the monk has never wished to name.

We have already seen this in Karl Popper. The American writer, David Riesman, is another example. He believes that our loss of faith in political solutions, rather than driving us to some other form of religiosity should encourage us to develop the 'nerve of failure'. It is certainly good not to be broken by failure, but Riesman is a generation behind; like all intellectuals he is thinking historically, he is thinking of the Koestlers and the Silones and has forgotten that another failure on the scale of that which occurred between the wars will be the last. If fascism comes to America, the intellectuals will have failed *for the last time*. As evident as this appears, Riesman cannot have realized it, for in *Individualism Reconsidered* he twice speaks with cheerful aplomb not of the possibility but the probability of failure.[2] Riesman carries to an almost ludicrous extreme the scholar's refusal to conclude,[3] a process which, rather than 'objec-

---

[1] This has come at the worst possible moment, because it is *our* intransigence or our willingness to compromise that will weaken or strengthen the current of liberalism in communist countries which has come into being since the death of Stalin. Unfortunately for all of us, the acquisitive society could not have a more dangerous enemy than a liberalized communism.

[2] Doubleday Anchor Books, 1955, pp. 38 and 80.

[3] Ibid. See, for example, p. 133. Riesman even goes so far as to advise intellectuals to have the '. . . courage not to take a stand'! (p. 119).

tive', he prefers to call 'dialectic' and which in his writing amounts to the so careful balancing of pros against cons that one is assured of getting nowhere despite the immensely increased dangers of this kind of irresponsibility.

Men like Popper and Riesman while giving lip service to constructive activity are in reality counsellors of despair, and if I have discussed them at some length, it is because their attitudes have become popular and because it is vitally important for us to get beyond this stage of barren disillusionment with political absolutes. We must get our society back on to the road again, we must open up a future for it, and in this task the objective intellectual can be of no use because he refuses to believe we can go forward without the help of fanaticism.

The 'mind-body problem' like most problems of philosophy does not present itself spontaneously—it is part of the game of stopping the arrow in mid-flight. The question, how can the mental affect the physical, *assumes* a separation for which evidence had originally to be painstakingly gathered, and today it has become possible, indeed essential, to build up evidence in support of the opposite view. Ostensibly, of course, modern philosophy has been applying itself to this very task, but it does so as the christian strives for the suppression of Evil; if he succeeded, his system would collapse, and the only way, if not to succeed, at least to progress further, is to stop being an orthodox christian. The imaginary entities Good and Evil are there to 'clarify', to comfort, to make decision effortless, and the same may be said of matter and mind which, apart from scientific rationalism, are no more conceivable separated from one another than are language and thought. If Good is also Evil, as pacifism in the democracies was evil between the wars, and if thought is also participation, as the monk participates in reinforcing the rotting structure of capitalism and therefore in bringing closer the third and final world war, how are we to make careers of virtue or of thought? To begin to think outside the framework of the classical division into mind and body is, in the long run, to threaten thinking as a profession, much as marxism threatens property as an inalienable right. When, for example, Alain writes: 'Let us not say, therefore, that the experiment has as its goal the verification of a hypothesis, but rather that the hypothesis determines the fact', is he not, by thus blurring the sharp lines between body and mind, between fact and hypothesis, is he not, in the final analysis, making the thinker responsible for the

97

facts? Whitehead pushed into these dangerous waters when he wrote: 'Progress consists in modifying the laws of nature . . .' or again: 'When we examine the general world of occurrent fact, we find that its general character, practically inescapable, is neutral in respect to the realization of intrinsic value.'[1] Unlike Alain, Whitehead did not stop short at that, he was led on to say: 'The essence of freedom is the practicability of purpose', and therefore: 'In modern thought, the expression of this truth has taken the form of "the economic interpretation of history".'[2] The freedom of speech and press to which the monk attaches an absolutely vital importance, and of which he almost never makes use, any more than he makes use of his academic freedom, these Whitehead calls the 'frills' of freedom. In brief, what the Chinese are doing, is to be preferred to what we in the West are thinking. Whitehead might very well not have subscribed to this opinion, for he remained much attached to the 'persuasive' and therefore terribly slow embodiment of ideas in things. Nevertheless, by suggesting that thought need not be merely explanatory but should be creative, in the literal, physical sense, Whitehead helps break down the artificial distinction between idea and thing, which is the very foundation of the objective society. It is therefore not surprising that retarded rationalists like Popper should find Whitehead 'irrational'. Classical rationality consists in believing that ideas are *about* things, that things are 'pre-constituted', and the advance made by Popper's 'critical rationalism' is to deny that political Absolutes are pre-constituted. In this way the monk absolves us of the messianic duty toward, but fails to replace it by that of responsibility for, which follows from the understanding that ideas are not about things, they are constitutive of things. Present-day rationalism has achieved a degree of non-functionalism reminiscent of Victorian gothic—the nadir of western architecture.

Students of Marx are coming to attach an increasing importance to writings which preceded *Capital*, and in studying these writings one gets the impression that Marx was not a marxist because for him dialectical materialism, far from explaining the movement of history without recourse to the spiritual, accounts for such movement (which is therefore a progress, as in Whitehead) as the materialization of idea—the changes man brings about in pursuing his goals. Marxism denies existence to the spiritual only in so far as its purpose is revealed as impracticable. Virtue and idea (to the extent in which it

[1] *Adventures of Ideas*, Cambridge, 1933, p. 53.   [2] Ibid., p. 84.

is contemplative or objective) are not 'wrong', they are powerless. The machiavellism of Marx consists simply in noting that unarmed virtue is little better than none at all, that mind apart from body (as, ultimately, in Hegel) is pure wish-fulfilment.

The second thesis on Feuerbach reads as follows: 'The question whether objective truth can be attributed to human thinking is not a question of theory—but is a practical question. In practice, man must prove the truth, that is, the reality and power, the this-sidedness of his thinking. The dispute over the reality or non-reality of thinking which is isolated from practice is a purely scholastic question.' Most of the other ten theses are in much this vein. '*In practice man must prove the truth.*' Marxism as a science is dead, as an instrument of progress it is not yet even understood. For example, in *The Meaning of Marxism*, G. D. H. Cole writes: 'The fact of class comes first, and the consciousness of class is secondary to it, for always and everywhere a thing must exist before men can become conscious of it.' This is pure classical rationalism. Not only are material things pre-constituted, but also social phenomena. Cole certainly does not consider marxism to be a science; and yet, if 'a thing must exist before men can become conscious of it', it is difficult to see why marxism (or some related system) should not be a science, since the object of enquiry is safely and securely in existence before consciousness has had a chance to deform it; it is born in complete independence of man and is consequently either the product of natural law, or meaningless.

We are perfectly justified in talking about social class before the first stirrings of class consciousness but only if we bear in mind that a social class like everything else is at once subjective and objective. Subjective, because the conception of class did not exist before a given historical moment, and it would therefore be absurd to reproach Saint-Simon for being a snob; objective, because class is something the existence of which marxism has 'proven' by constituting for us a historical perspective in which the notion of class, because it has been practically effective, is productive of meaning. To the distress of the orthodox rationalist, whose thirst for clarity has become a camouflage for defeatism, we must therefore say that while Saint-Simon cannot be criticized for his social attitudes, we not only can, but should find them objectionable. A man's whole life will inevitably be interpreted in the light of what he eventually became. A childhood theft will become either the first

99

step toward perdition or an amusing anecdote in the life of a prominent man. But at the time it was committed, the theft was neither one nor the other. At one and the same time, that childhood act was and was not a disastrous mistake. The prominent man is free to 'prove' at any moment, by an embezzlement for example, that what he did as a child, far from being a mere vagary was, in fact, evidence of an 'inherent corruption', which finally gained the upper hand. So with history. Lenin 'proved' Marx to be right.

History *has* a meaning, but it is one we create, one which we 'prove', one for which we, the intellectuals, are responsible.

For centuries, we have believed that to know was to be able. In our science-dominated philosophy, the act of the highest efficacy is the act of knowing. But now we see the reverse to be true; it is act which makes knowledge possible, whether it be an act of consciousness which is not a judgement but an 'incredible simplification' as Whitehead calls it, that is, a 'choice', or whether it be a five-year plan the success of which will help to 'prove' the marxist interpretation of history.

The 'pre-constituted' world of classical thinking, 'discovered' by thought and unaffected by act in the sense of choice is of necessity a hidden one, otherwise it crumbles away. When primitive peoples make musical instruments out of abandoned petrol containers, how can we continue to regard the object as a container unless some hidden essence guarantees its identity? In reality, of course, the native has not failed to recognize an object for what it is, he has reconstituted it; he has incorporated it into a perspective in which it is as much a musical instrument as is a violin for us. The reality of objects, in other words, is what is most evident about them—their use. Appearances are deceptive only in so far as we regard the exterior world as an object of thought rather than as the milieu in which we exist. It is in this context that the underlying oneness of the objective and acquisitive societies is most easily appreciated. Just as for the 'essentialist' thinker, the identity of an object (which is hidden since it survives all possible metamorphoses) precedes and determines its use, so for the capitalist, the reality of a commodity is not its use, but its price, fixed by mysterious and impersonal agencies, as the identities of objects were fixed before there were men, and consequently without consulting them. If reality is hidden, then scholars are performing the most vital of all tasks, that of seeking it out; if the value (or reality) of a commodity is its price, then the capitalist also, who deals in prices and only incidentally in goods, performs a vital service. The stock market resembles nothing so much as our 'halls of learning' where false values are busily exchanged in complete isolation from the needs and realities of daily life. If, however, reality is constituted and not disclosed, and if the value of a commodity is not its price but its usefulness,[1] then we can dispense with both the scholar and the capitalist in so far as they persist in regarding their function as one which 'realizes an essence'. It seems absurd to say that the essence of a commodity is its price, yet capitalism is founded upon just this absurdity because it permits the employer to suppose that since it is he who pays for the commodity known as labour, it is in him that value finds its origin. If the value of a worker may be fully expressed in the form of a wage (however high), then the capitalist is the very keystone of our social structure. But if, which of course is the case, a man is more than his wage; if, to use Marx's term, labour, like every other commodity, has a use-value, then it is this use-value which is at the source of all others, its use is to *create* value. This is the hard core of marxism which time cannot touch. Man is the unique source of value,[2] and the economics of supply and demand is an attempt to reintroduce the supra-human. An article is not valuable because it is scarce, it is scarce because it is valuable, because men have placed a value upon it.

The philosophy of Marx deviated into scientism because the first concern of most marxists was to demonstrate how means of production had 'determined' the nature of all other manifestations of social life throughout human history. This was to forget that man can create value not only with his hands, but also with his mind. The economic interpretation of history is proven not by consulting the records, but by turning this thought into matter. The thinker, in other words, is a labourer, except that his product is an event or an

[1] In the great majority of cases, a saleable article is, of course, also a useful one. But this does not alter the fact that the capitalists' first concern is sale, not utility; and it is increasingly the goal of advertising not to explain the utility of an article, but to create a need for it. That nature from which the objective thinker distils its truths, which are in reality *his* truths, is the one from which the capitalist wrings its profits, which are in reality *his* profits.

[2] Theoretically, this is the position of the humanists; but in practice, they have for long ceased to create value and now simply transmit it. They are prisoners of culture as possession and their occasional disputes with the faithful give the sound of an eighteenth-century music box with its unchanging and unchangeable melodies constantly being drowned out by the roar of traffic.

institution rather than a commodity. For the objective intellectual, at least in practice, ideas and things run parallel to one another; but the lines can be made to cross, and, indeed, the whole responsibility of the intellectual is to see that they do. The marxists (and the freudians) have developed the maddening practice of evaluating an idea on the basis of its origin, the bourgeois thinker is alleged to be secretly motivated by class interest. But the objective intellectual does precisely the same thing when he refuses to discuss a statement on the grounds that it is marxist or on the grounds that it is 'metaphysical'. The intellectual has grown so used to his ineffectualness, and so reconciled to it, that he is shocked by the suggestion that ideas, like things, have use-values, and that again like things, they wear out and must be replaced.

We will therefore say that the value of an idea depends upon what it tries to accomplish plus the practical possibility of such accomplishment. There was no difficulty about what marxism was to try to accomplish, it was to carry on the work of the eighteenth century and of the French revolution; it was to push on with the work of liberating men from one another. But in the domain of practical possibility everything remained to be done. The seizure of power by the middle classes had taken centuries, Marx hoped to reduce this, in the case of the proletariat, to a matter of years; and, in order to do so, the most pressing need was to create in the masses (still largely illiterate) a sense of solidarity and of mission. The retrograde messianic element of marxism did just this. It was a question of practical necessity. The bourgeosie had had the immense advantages of economic power and education, the workers had nothing but their faith or their fanaticism. I am not suggesting that the 'real' Marx is the philosopher of the *Theses on Feuerbach* rather than the 'scientist' of *Capital*. The point is that not only was Marx both these men, but for reasons of practical effectiveness he was forced to be both of them. If anything at all were to be accomplished, it had to be the inevitable. The idea of a 'manifest destiny' of the masses gave moral stature to marxism as a technique of revolution; a moral stature without which a revolution is a mere *coup d'état*. Marxism appeals to history as the bourgeoisie appealed to Reason.

In so far as it has humanized capitalism, marxism may be said to have succeeded in the west as well as elsewhere. Whether such compromises as the New Deal and the Welfare State have been in reality catastrophes for marxism is an idle question. It is usually foolish to give up an existent good for a conjectural better; but it is equally foolish to make of an actual good a permanent resting place. Poverty is not our only political problem and messianism was no more fundamental to marxism than was the inquisition to christianity.

The quasi-sciences like psycho-analysis and sociology are manifestations of the society upon which they propose to sit in judgement and which they propose to help. Freudism was largely an attempt to counteract sexual frustration, which is not a characteristic of the human animal, but the product of a given society. Its only permanent cure will be political. The sociologist works within the framework of a given political system. He is a tool. At best he can propose, others will dispose. The fundamental reality in what concerns man is always decision, not fact. In the foreseeable future the vital decisions will be political; and, at the moment, apart from marxism, there is no possibility of giving these decisions a constructive and progressive coherence.

Certain reconsiderations are nevertheless forced upon us. First, because extremes of poverty no longer appear, for the moment, to be an inevitable concomitant of capitalism (except in fascist countries unable to prepare for war, like Spain and Portugal); the most obvious and pressing need for marxism has, therefore, disappeared, at least in the Anglo-Saxon countries. Secondly, in part as a result of this, marxism as a faith, that is, as a practical possibility, is much diminished.

There is little left of illiteracy in the broad sense of superstitious gullibility among the masses of the people in the west, and one of the most surprising developments of our time is its reappearance in a conscious form among the educated. This is true not only of the great number of latter-day believers, but also of many communist intellectuals who, especially in the French and British parties, have proved to be more stalinist than the Russians themselves. The Hungarian revolution seems to have shaken the masses more than the leaders. This suppression of illiteracy among the workers is a comparatively recent happening, and one to which we have perhaps not yet adjusted our thinking. It means that the masses have acceded to that healthy scepticism of classical rationalism for which the believer has substituted an *ersatz* medievalism and which the unregenerate communist despises as bourgeois.[1] Above all, it means that practical

[1] The only way I can account for the tone of sentimental paternalism one finds in some communist publications, especially *l'Humanité*, is to suppose that they are still being addressed to the nineteenth-century illiterate worker.

accomplishment is no longer dependent upon messianism of one form or another; and where blind enthusiasm occurs among literate masses as in fascism, the goal is not primarily material achievement, but spiritual comfort. In fascism, the loathsome bourgeois thirst for status poisons the entire body politic including a portion of the intellectuals. But this is a matter to which we shall return in a moment.

What is best in the scientific attitude is also what is most rudimentary in it, a hesitancy to believe just anything; and the broad dissemination of this characteristic which has followed the suppression of absolute illiteracy offers man one of the great opportunities in his history—the doing away with tutelage (which was still vital to the Russians at the beginning of the Bolshevic revolution), the final abolition of the Shamans. The masses no longer need to be led, all they require is to be protected from mystification, and the most subtly damaging of these at present is the conception of culture which prevails in our society. Culture as something we acquire rather than something we do is a mystification. Far from bringing us closer to some higher form of humanity (as the eighteenth-century rationalist may be said to represent a higher form than his ecclesiastical opponent), it establishes a kind of caste system, since a good majority of university students are quite unable to take on the slightest tincture of what their teachers would consider to be culture; often, I think, because of a psychological good health which makes them independent of a commodity whose function, when it is not that of improving social status, is frequently to compensate for some maladjustment to one's times or one's fellows. It is sufficient to consider any group of academics concerned with teaching the humanities to understand that happiness or serenity is no more to be attained in this way than in any other way unrelated to constructive action; indeed, soliloquies like those of Browning's Spanish monk cannot be uncommon among men who are always so 'disappointed' with one another's work which, where it must be admitted to be 'stimulating' and 'provocative' is for that very reason 'unsound'. The thought of an entire population raised through culture to the morose dignity of an arts faculty is terrifying; and luckily, pure fancy. We are tirelessly warned against the great danger of increasing the scientific content of our education at the expense of the humanities. But this is simply one of the ways in which the objective intellectual turns his back upon his very heavy responsibilities to the nation and to mankind. He would have us believe that if the world is going to pot it is because people are no longer interested in culture and not because the intellectual is failing to do his work. We have seen that culture, like religion, offers salvation to the individual. But of a society's élite, it is the scientists, the engineers and doctors, those whose work requires that the individual be sacrificed to the collective effort whose lives, rather than those of the intellectuals, offer us examples of sound happiness. It is not the technician who needs culture; it is the intellectual who needs a sense of purpose.

The situation is this: messianism of whatever description is no longer politically necessary nor intellectually acceptable; on the other hand, it is only through habit that the monk goes on waiting for the Venus of Truth to emerge full-blown out of the sea of learning. The preaching of culture as possession is hopelessly remote from the realities of the moment. We are, therefore, faced by the urgent necessity of restoring the possibility of constructive political action; and, bearing in mind artistic and philosophical developments of the past fifty years, this can best be done by coming to understand that truth is not hidden, but evident. It is not uncovered by a long and complex process of reasoning; it is already there, and the vital point is no longer knowledge or ignorance but, in the case of the intellectual, how will he react, what will he do.

Meaning is inherent in existence itself. In some parts of the world it is possible to feel quite comfortable out in the air where the thermometer registers 90 degrees. Some people, upon seeing the thermometer, will immediately feel warmer (a good example of the way in which the mental constitutes the physical) but most will adjust themselves to the temperature they *feel*, not to the one they *know*. No one would argue that 90 degrees is the 'real' temperature and that consequently we should feel uncomfortably warm. The real temperature is the one we 'exist', the measured one having been invented for specific purposes; and the same may be said for codes of ethics or systems of philosophy which purport to be definitive, they answer deep-lying psychological purposes, but have little or nothing to do with existence, except in so far as they develop into fanaticism. The cubist paints what he 'exists', since he paints what he sees rather than what he thinks; and if what he sees appears to us anything but evident it is because we are unaware of the extent to which unconscious intellection alters the scene before us, and to depict it as it is 'existed' may require a kind of discipline, what, on

105

the philosophical level, the phenomenologists call a 'reduction'. What we see in the face of a person coming toward us is its gaiety, its sorrow, its fear, etc. We do not see the features of the face as such unless, for one reason or another, we wish to scrutinize the person's face as a face; unless, that is, we abstract it from its existential context. Why, then, should not the artist try to seize this expression, and if the face becomes unrecognizable in the process, it is because to avoid this the painter would have had to make a specific act of observation which would have led him not closer to reality but farther from it. We have already remarked that analysis leads not to the 'fundamental' but to the different. It is the same with language. In ordinary circumstances we always know what people mean when they speak to us. Trouble begins with the philosopher and his definitions. In a philosophical discussion, of course, terms must be defined; but this is because philosophers have a language of their own and one which is not a scientific terminology. Nothing is more superfluous than definitions for everyday language. The word 'democracy' may be abused by a given political régime, but everyone knows perfectly well that it is being abused, and when the philosopher suggests as a *practical measure* (as he is capable of doing) a more severe attention to what we mean by the words we use, then we can only regret not hearing from him on such occasions as the royal visit to a country which, at the time, was officially designated as the 'Republic' of Portugal. It will not do to say that this is a job for the newspapermen. Today we can no more afford to leave these matters to the newspapers than we can afford to leave war to the military.

The truth is evident in the sense that it always gives the impression of having been there right along waiting for us to open our eyes to it or turn ourselves in its direction. Great artists 'reveal' it in the world around us, as the cubist reveals to us that we always see a square table as square from whatever angle we view it. It is science, of course, that has misled us here; but once we have understood that the province of science is measurement and not the Truth, we see that the latter may be compared to the scene we look out upon through a window. It is inescapably there, and yet it is enough to fix our eyes upon a mark in the glass to cause it to almost disappear. The specks and scratches on the glass are innumerable, and each can be a pretext for looking at the glass rather than through it. It is for this reason that argument is futile. The man who 'cannot' see the street through the window is not stupid, he has wilfully focused his eyes differently; it is this which enables selfish or corrupt public servants to remain 'honourable' men. Except for the misinformed or the mentally sluggish, no one ever 'sees the light'. It is absurd to suppose that when the literate catholic declares his opposition to birth control, or when the South African legislates against non-whites, that these people are 'mistaken'—they have deliberately focused their eyes upon the glass, and talk of enlightenment or of reason is not to the point. The work of the intellectual, therefore, is not to enlighten, but to combat.

A paradox is often a platitude turned inside out. The truth is not what we 'attain', it is the element we live in, it is what makes attainment possible; it is not a comfort, but a summons. There is an intellectual as well as a physical debauchery—it consists in deflowering a multitude of ideas because the virility necessary to the full utilization of one or two is lacking. The Don Juan has little to offer, so he is absorbed in taking. The true thinker is a man of few ideas; these ideas in some elemental form will be the property of every literate reasonably informed person, *because it is only this kind of idea that one can hope to implement*, and the man unconcerned about implementing his thought is not a thinker, he is a mere collector of ideas.

To talk of implementing one's ideas on any significant scale is to talk of one form or another of marxism, and this will be so until the economic structure of the west has been permanently and fundamentally altered. The diffusion of marxist ideas is such that its bitterest opponents live by them. What conservative government would dare conduct itself as conservatively as it would like? Capitalist democracy is that extraordinary form of government in which, because of the weight of popular sentiment, real political power must be exercised as much as possible in secret. Money is like a gravitational pull, its influence is invisible but omnipotent. It will not do to say that it is democratic sentiment which forces the power of money into clandestinity, because a form of government in which this power no longer existed would not be democracy as we know it, it would be a form of marxism (or, conceivably, a form of fascism—the choice is ours). In other words, democracy fully implemented is marxism. The capitalist democracy that would at last and somehow be genuinely democratic is part of the monk's dream world.[1]

[1] The anti-marxist intellectual will reply that he is a 'realist', that there is a better chance of improving democracy as it exists than of establishing society on

We have reached the stage where it has become a discipline to ignore the obvious, because acknowledging it at once invokes the embarrassing genie of marxism. Is it not, for example, peculiar that middle-class attitudes should be held by the nation's intelligentsia to be beneath contempt, and that they should, at the same time, dominate our way of life? No self-respecting person of any education could accept himself as a typical representative of middle-class culture. The word 'bourgeois' in France is all but an insult. It is presposterous that for a century and a half the bourgeois's uniquely inglorious set of values should have been under constant attack and yet should flourish today as never before. The intellectual is not only ready but eager to cite this as an example of his impotence; it is, of course, an example of his choice of impotence, which takes the form of a manifestly futile search for means other than political, that is other than marxist, for ridding us of middle-class domination.

If it is true, as I have been contending, that conduct is always to a very considerable extent a matter of choice, that wrong-doing is in no essential way connected with ignorance, then our problem is to explain why people look at the window rather than through it, why the evident carries no compulsion. This is the great problem of our time—it is at one extreme that of fascism, at the other, that of finding out why a section of the working class in this country votes for a party which admits that it is conservative. The extent in which marxism has failed to account for fascism (although the marxist interpretation is the only one which comes anywhere near to being satisfactory) is the extent in which the working class has revealed itself prepared to co-operate with its enemies. In exchange for what? This has turned out to be Marx's most serious miscalculation; rather than the increasing accentuation of class differences which he foresaw, the reverse has come about. If we are to develop marxism, then clearly we ought to begin here.

To be more specific, what needs to be developed is Marx's conception of 'alienation', because there has come into being a new kind of alienation (which has gone furthest in America) to which, this time, the workers themselves have more or less consented.

It will be recalled that the bed-rock of marxism is the principle

a different basis. But history is change, and democracy is not going to evolve unless it evolves into something else. As far as the 'realism' of the bourgeois intellectual is concerned, it is he who suggests culture as a practical remedy for the ills of the time.

according to which all value issues from man. Alienation is simply the violation of that principle. Let me quote from *Capital* one of the many passages in which Marx explains how this occurs under capitalism. He calls capitalism a '. . . mode of production in which the labourer exists to satisfy the needs of self-expansion of existing values, instead of, on the contrary, material wealth existing to satisfy the needs of development on the part of the labourer. As, in religion, man is governed by the products of his own brain, so, in capitalistic production, he is governed by the products of his own hands.' In reading this today one thinks inevitably of America and, to a lesser degree, of western Europe (always assuming, of course, which is anything but certain, that modern capitalism has learned to control recurrent economic depression). Nevertheless, the worker is still 'governed by the products of his own hands', but in a way very different from that Marx had in mind.

Rather than the gradual elimination of economic groups rising from the proletariat to the bourgeoisie, we have seen their proliferation; or, to put this in another way, the immense productivity of modern industry has made it possible, for almost anyone who earnestly wishes it, to accede to respectability. Class is coming to depend less upon what one owns than upon a state of mind; it is increasingly a matter of choice, but since there is no proletarian culture there is, in reality, no choice except to move 'up', and one appreciates here the immensity of the intellectuals' betrayal—as the only practicable moral code, the masses have been left with the most pitiable of them all, bourgeois respectability; as the only culture, the most barren of them all, that of the pseudo-scientist.

Except for those on the right side of the fence, the class struggle is still very real, especially, of course, in the latin countries. Nevertheless, the improvement in conditions of working-class life, and the criminal blunders of stalinist politics have cut deeply into the cohesion and combativeness of the masses. The traditional working-class way of life is rapidly becoming an object of historical curiosity, and it would seem that what we need now is to change from the scientific or pseudo-scientific conception of man as a *product* (of class, sociological 'law', etc.) to the ontological conception of man as a being in himself. We must turn to what Sartre calls 'human reality' and to the philosophy of Sartre himself for it is here that we shall find the most help in our efforts to interpret and to control what is happening.

109

If thought is inconceivable apart from language, intuition is not. Intuition is at once knowledge, and speechless. Great philosophies begin as intuitions which the philosopher must try to put into language. The result is usually a jungle of words through which the first unfortunate readers hack their way step by step; but it is the language, not the intuition which is difficult.[1] I am going to try to reduce the difficulty of Sartre's *Being and Nothingness* by simplifying the language. Our object will be to get at the intuition which underlies the argument in the expectation that it will be of a nature not only to help toward the renovation of marxism, but to provide further evidence for the homogeniety of modern art and the trend of thought we are pursuing, which would be the best guarantee that we are dealing with what is, and not with what happens to please us. For Marx, Hegel was an inspiration, but Balzac was a guarantee.

The denial of human progress is a philosophical nicety. By progress, I mean progress in the way in which we treat our fellows. What we should not forget about nazi and stalinist atrocities is precisely that they were or are so termed by virtually everyone. Régimes that might once have lasted centuries now have a much briefer existence. The horror of the concentration camps marks not an increase in human viciousness, but an increase in technical and organizational efficiency. The very magnitude of nazi crimes suggests an attempt to achieve the thrill that accompanies deliberate wrongdoing. We are dealing with a 'black mass' mentality, and at a black mass the presence of God is more indispensable than that of the Devil.

Our progress has been measured by the ever-increasing inclusiveness of what we regard as inadmissible or outrageous. The monk will often look back to the Enlightenment as to a kind of golden age; it was also an age in which, in parts of western Europe, miners went into the pits on Monday morning not to emerge again until the

[1] The difference between literature and philosophy is one of degree, not of kind. It depends upon the degree of comprehensiveness to which the particular intuition lays claim. The intuitions of philosophy aspire to be all inclusive and are hence extremely difficult to express; while those of literature, being concerned with 'local', everyday truth, can make use of plainer language. We know that most great literature is remarkable for its simplicity of expression, but it would seem (except, sometimes, where centuries have turned obscurity into clarity, like a path worn smooth) that in philosophy this may well indicate superficiality. The language of much current Anglo-Saxon philosophy is neither difficult nor simple, but esoteric, like that of astrology—a discipline with which it has other points in common.

following Saturday. It was an age in which the guides at Vesuvius were equipped with straps with which to pull distinguished travellers up the slopes so that they might peer into the crater. I think that today the conversion of a fellow human being into a draught animal would make most of us uncomfortable; it did not in the least disturb Goethe who, in his *Italian Journey*, tells of being helped to the summit in this way. Antiquity comes to us through the golden mists of a Claude Lorrain—we neither see nor hear the watchdogs of Rome, who were not dogs at all but human beings chained to the door. There is no progress of the mind, no one thinks more power-fully than did the Greeks; but there has been progress in those things upon which we turn our minds; or, as Hegel would have put it, in those things which consciousness brings into being. There is therefore a respect in which the most mediocre among us represents a progress over the greatest of the Greeks—for us slavery is an abomination and racism often incomprehensible; for the Greeks, the question did not yet even exist.

In trying to understand the nature of this progress, we must beware of the catch words—humanism, individualism, respect for the rights of the individual, etc. Our analyses of the renaissance individual, of bourgeois culture, of the mentality of the monk, have revealed these conceptions to be camouflaged irrelevancies. The renaissance aristocrat and the cultivated gentleman of bourgeois society are not essentially 'free' individuals, they are essentially functions, the embodiments of an Order of which, along with the police, the humanists and the academics are the keepers; or, more recently, in conjunction with certain literary men, the hired mourners. The emerging of the individual with the renaissance comes about, as we have seen, because communication with the supra-human is now effected with the mind rather than the senses; that is, the individual attains a new importance inasmuch as vast and vital domains of knowledge have appeared which, however, are not accessible to man by the mere fact of his being a christian in possession of all his senses, but which require the attention of a penetrating and highly trained or cultivated mind. In the middle ages, knowledge was essentially an a priori elucidation, not a discovery. The feudal lord therefore could safely be as 'ignorant' as his serfs since, in any case, there was nothing indispensable to be known which God had not made readily available to all. It is with the renaissance that ignorance becomes shameful because there is so much to be known, and apart from such

111

knowledge the 'good life' is unattainable. This situation persists into modern bourgeois civilization with its perpetual lamentations over the abysmal cultural level of the masses, over the abominal tastes of the 'reading public'. But the conception of freedom which accompanies culture envisaged in this way (as the one truly precious possession) has little or nothing to do with man's treatment of his fellows, in other words, with that progress whose nature we are trying to understand. The freedom of the cultivated man is that of the stoics—one is 'free' to the extent in which one is able to bring one's wishes into accord with the inexorable universe. Culture makes us independent of cruel circumstance, and it receives its noblest expression in the soldier reading Thomas Browne or Jane Austen in a shell-hole, even though this may bring about an inattention causing him to be buried alive with the next explosion. It is expressed in Koestler's 'let us build oases', which is to say, 'let us accept our defeat', for in that way it will cease to be a defeat. But where Marcus Aurelius succeeded, the modern stoic fails because he is retrograde. With the coming of marxism,[1] the nature of things ceased to be 'inexorable', and resignation therefore ceased to be a virtue.

Progress in man's treatment of man appears to be very closely associated with the slow break-down of all positive identifications of the nature of the universe. Between the earliest times and the Enlightenment, progress was slight, but it becomes easily perceptible during the age of *criticism*, the great rationalist age of the monk which could devote so much of its energies to the destruction of a system because it was unencumbered by one of its own. When rationalism did eventually acquire a fixed system in marxism (as the result of a *malentendu*), it lost no time in becoming oppressive.

Man's inhumanity to his fellows seems to depend upon the extent to which he can succeed in regarding them as objects—objects which, in certain historical circumstances, may come to be identified with precision and which therefore may be manipulated. This is one of the functions of religious and political Absolutes, to make it possible to govern by the manipulation of objects rather than by the consultation of subjects. Others are approached via the means of identifying them rather than directly; as things to be judged rather than as

[1] By which I mean, of course, a marxism in which the *Theses on Feuerbach* and various other earlier writings are given their full weight; the marxism of Marx as opposed to the atavistic messianism of what has been allowed to pass for marxism.

subjectivities with needs to be satisfied. The simplest illustration here of course is racism, for which a person may be not essentially another man (with all that that should imply for our conduct towards him) but essentially a colour, essentially an identifiable *thing*. Again, for the marxist bigot, the bourgeois is a historical thing which can do little to overcome his inherent viciousness. If he is a writer, then it will not be necessary to examine his work which will be of necessity corrupt. Even when the intention is of the best, 'objectively' the result will be harmful to the movement. As for the 'free world', no one who has passed a Sunday in a protestant community, or tried, apart from matrimony to give to fornication the exalted and time-consuming place in his life which it so richly deserves, or dared, if he is an academic, to say exactly what he thought to his students, no such person can suppose for a moment that he is a free agent rather than a damned object. The difference between east and west is that in the east tyranny is exercised by a bureaucracy, in the west by a good part of the population, including the intellectuals.

To discuss messianic absolutism, therefore, without coming to this reification of subjectivity (upon which all tyranny is based) is to ignore half the issue. In the case of the monk, subjectivity exists as a thing, but it is unidentified with any precision; and this is as we should expect since the Absolute itself is unidentified, though necessarily real if the work of the monk is to be satisfactorily justified. The parallel here is striking, for just as the monk can deny the existence of system or of an Absolute and yet (by his abstentionism) conduct himself as though they existed, so he may deny that man is object rather than subject, and yet his entire intellectual heritage, that of scientific rationalism, would be unthinkable apart from the conception of man as an animal which attains truth by the exercise of an object, the intellect, rather than one which receives it (with suitable alterations in our conception of the nature of truth) as a subject through consciousness. The notion of mind as a piece of machinery (and as that which distinguishes the human from the animal) for sifting the evidence of the senses, although an arbitrary assumption and not a discovered fact, is fundamental to our thinking. Here we need only bear in mind the usual procedure in psychological investigation which involves treating persons under observation as much as possible like objects. This is to forget that human beings are 'objects' which exist *for themselves* as well as for others, and that these two forms of existence are quite different; the classical example being the inverted image on the eye retina—inverted for the investigator, right side up for the subject. One of the marvels of our culture is the comfortable contempt with which we regard scientism, along with the immense influence it still wields. The very essence of scientism is to suppose the human animal accessible, like an object, from the outside; yet much of psychology and sociology is based upon precisely this assumption. Valuable information admittedly is to be gained in this way; but apart from the purely technical impasse into which scientism has led psychology, and which we cannot go into here,[1] we should appreciate that psychologists and sociologists, in forgetting that what they study is in part themselves, are carrying on the old conception (of which solipsism is the philosophical *reductio ad absurdum*) of man as a kind of Leibnitzian monad with neither doors nor windows, identified and operated upon entirely from without. Unless their society has beaten them into submission, the negro is not *for himself* a black man, the homosexual is not *for himself* 'abnormal', the 'sinner' is not *for himself* a wrong-doer. Similarly, when the psychologist or sociologist urges the individual to accept society's judgement upon him as being more valid than his own, they are exercising a subtle but terribly dangerous form of tyranny.

It is evident to most of us that this 'objectification' of man for the purpose of reconciling him to his social environment is a disaster;[2] what is less evident is that the only remedy envisaged by any Anglo-Saxon thinker is an obsolete form of the same ill, for the 'autonomous' individual of the past (Riesman's 'inner-directed' individual) does not offer us an effective alternative, but simply another means of achieving exactly the same goal as that of the modern 'other-directed' nonentity—the manufacture of a self along lines laid down by the dominating ethos. The conformist is not interested in 'losing himself' in the group, on the contrary, what he is after is a convenient means of self-identification, he 'finds peace' by accepting that image

[1] Had Merleau Ponty's work *La Structure du Comportement* (which appeared in 1943) been a book on physics, its impact would have been immediate and far-reaching. It has remained, if not unknown, then almost entirely without influence upon the study of psychology in Anglo-Saxon countries—a remarkable illustration of how far removed psychology is from being a science in the strict sense of the word.

[2] Need it be pointed out that the difference between stalinist tyranny and the insidious pressure exercised by a group abetted by the scientism of the sociologist is one of degree and not of kind, since both forms of oppression derive from belief in the irrelevance of subjective needs.

114

of himself proposed by the group to which he belongs. With man's eternal question 'Who am I?' he turns to the group, where the 'inner-directed' individual turned toward those absolutes we associate with the protestant industrial culture of the last century and which produced some of the most repulsive human types known to history—precisely because we have in these individuals the minimum expression of subjectivity, the maximum suppression of the 'merely human', a degree of self-discipline which so warped the old Adam that Freud came as a natural sequel. The only truly 'inner-directed' individuals are those who resist both the pressure of the group and that of, in the final analysis, *other* imposed notions of what they 'owe themselves'—but these are the people society casts out, the beach-combers, the revolutionaries, the geniuses.

Sartre has remarked that all present-day attempts at non-marxist thinking invariably turn out to be revivals of some form of pre-marxist thinking. Sociology, for example, has eliminated the idea of historical evolution that one would have supposed a permanent and precious heritage from the nineteenth century. Riesman seems completely undisturbed by the fact that history has carried away his 'inner-directed' individual,[1] and that the men in whom traces of him are still to be found—the monk, the messiah, the 'cultivated' gentleman—are studies in futility as far as society at large is concerned. We have seen how (using the example of Karl Popper) western society and government as they are now constituted have come to be regarded by the monk as being that Absolute which he had previously not cared to name—we do not need to improve our society (that would be marxism), we need to protect it. It is this immutable, a-historical, directionless object that the sociologist studies. Perhaps the sociologist, who is the more or less unconscious servant of the 'power élite',[2] conceives the group in this way because western thought has now reached the dangerous stage where it has become practicable to regard it (in the case of the social class)

---

[1] As well he might be of course since like every self-respecting Anglo-Saxon intellectual he has nothing whatever to advocate. This is so because no great philosophy (one that affects our lives, as science does) is pulled out of a hat; it 'grows up' and makes philosophers as much as philosophers make it. Consequently Sartre does not consider that his philosophy supplants that of Marx, it supplements it.

[2] In a B.B.C. programme about mental illnesses and the lost man-hours they cost industry, a lecturer in industrial relations explained that, along with tea breaks, strikes are a 'method of avoiding work'!

primarily as an *enterprise for the transformation of reality*.[1] At the present moment it is only by thinking along these lines that we shall progress further toward the total liberation of man from man.

There should be no difficulty at this point about accepting reality not as something we discover but as something we create in the sense of attaching a significance to.[2] Prior to the intervention of human consciousness, matter is to be looked upon as utterly meaningless, or 'absurd', and this is what Sartre (to whose philosophy we may now turn) calls the in-itself. Thus at the outset we do away with those 'eternal truths' (which the christian existentialist tries to retain while keeping abreast of the latest developments in philosophy) that men have manufactured through the ages but which they prefer to believe 'revealed' or 'discovered' so that, from time to time, they may be invoked to justify the most outrageous enterprises against human dignity and freedom.[3]

We cannot take as radical a step as this without, at the same time, undertaking to rethink our entire conception of 'human reality'. If we are going to deny that there is an all-inclusive principle of Order, then we observe at once that: (1) the world is nevertheless full of what are increasingly coming to be called 'structures' (of civilizations, primitive societies, cultures, etc.); and (2) these areas of meaning or significance are far too shifting and complex for us to conceive them as being mere projections of the mind in the fashion of the idealists; but (3) since we posit an 'absurd' universe, where can these regional schemes of order come from if not from man himself considered not as a thing (either as the product of a supreme Order or as 'containing' that Order in his mind—in this context it is

[1] In *A Piece of my Mind*, Edmund Wilson tells of the man who, applying for American citizenship, was asked, somewhat menacingly, whether he thought it was possible 'to make the world a better place to live in'. This is much more than an expression of bureaucratic imbecility, it is the conviction implicit in the work of occidental sociology which is about all we have at present in the way of 'political thought'.

[2] Science itself has moved close to this view. Toward the end of his book *Causality and Chance in Modern Physics*, David Bohm argues that physics should postulate a universe of 'inexhaustible diversity'. Science is creative in the sense that a knowledge of the whole (now regarded as unattainable) is no longer considered to be indispensable to effective knowledge of the parts, and we may apply to it the remark Gide made about himself: 'I don't know where I'm going, but I'm advancing.'

[3] Needless to say, this process was always quite unconscious until, as we have seen, the last century when rationalist humanitarian idealism came into conflict with 'sound' business practice. Marx turned *laissez faire* into a thin disguise for *laissez nous faire*.

all one) but as an activity. But if this is the case, if man is a *passing* from one thing to another and not himself a thing, then he must be a kind of 'nothingness', what Sartre calls the for-itself.

If these conceptions are to lose their air of paradox, we must accept the basic premise of existentialist as opposed to classical thinking; namely, that truth is those arrangements or patterns of things which man 'exists', which man as a purposeful activity has brought into being. Parts of chapter one may have prepared the reader for this notion. There we saw that the world of the middle ages was real in the sense of being actually perceived; and yet this world has quite disappeared, not because it was 'hallucinatory' but because it ceased to be 'existed'. Let me try to make this clearer by using the example of the individual. We have a tendency to suppose that joy or sorrow is something that 'happens to' a person; that it is a kind of more or less superficial 'coloration' temporarily assumed and that there is a central core or identity which remains untouched. One can think of the matter however in a very different way. Joy and sorrow (or any other emotion) are not entities, but ways in which it is possible to exist, they are modes of existence, so that joy *is* a given person at a given moment, and nothing more. It is a kind of comportment. In somewhat the same way the world is not what we passively experience, or 'happen upon', or 'discover' as, in the old psychology, passion was something that 'ruled' us. It can have no meaningful existence apart from that selective act by which we give significance to this and deny it to that. The world is what a collectivity exists. The world of geological time, as it was before man, exists *now*, *for us*, just as a memory does not take place in the past, it is something we do at this moment. The objective society, therefore, enquiring as to 'what, in fact, is the case', is not learning anything about a 'pre-given' world, it is 'existing' the world, that is, comporting itself, in a certain way, and in a way which is a luxury we can no longer afford. It is, in the marxian sense of the word, alienating itself. Just as the worker creates wealth which another appropriates, the objective thinker creates a world over which he prefers to think he has no control; as though it were 'ready made' and had to be put up with as it is.

We saw a moment ago that subjectivity, or what Sartre calls the for-itself, is a kind of nothingness. We now know more about it. It is the way in which things exist. Objects exist in as many ways as there are people to exist them. Two men may come to the same village, but if one of them is a travelling salesman, and if the other is returning after many years' absence to his childhood home, the village will exist in two entirely different ways; and it will be the same village only because it has a third form of existence—that which it has not for the individual in himself, but for the individual as a member of the collectivity. This is difficult for us to grasp because all our thinking, our perception even, relies unconsciously upon the conception of a world in which matter is at a distance from mind, the result being that philosophy is reduced to little more than epistemology. There is no solution to the 'problems of perception' except to deny that there are any by positing not a subjectivity in 'direct contact' with the material world, but one which is simply the way in which things exist.

Formerly it had to be considered that mind reasoned and judged its way to a more or less accurate knowledge of matter; but if we are going to argue that subjectivity is a 'mode of existence' of matter, knowledge will derive from consciousness, and the function of reason will not be to discover what we do not know, but to utilize what we do know. It will be recalled that scientific reason reveals other aspects of matter, it does not lead us to greater knowledge of the exterior world in the sense of leading slowly to some definitive formulation as to the 'real nature' of the world around us. Just as no one seeks Christ who has not already found him, the scientist has to know what he is looking for or he would never find it. In other words, as we have frequently had occasion to remark, the basic phenomenon is 'orientation', not discovery.

Up to the moment, we have regarded the for-itself as *being* the perceived object and nothing more. This may be verified by noticing that it is quite impossible to come to an awareness of anything in addition to that of which there is consciousness; in other words, consciousness is always consciousness of what is not itself—everything is exterior to the for-itself. Consequently, when the expression 'perceived object' is used it must be borne in mind that this refers not only to material objects, but to whatever there is consciousness of—a memory, a pain, etc. Hence Sartre's term 'in-itself' which is not matter as opposed to mind, but everything of which it is possible to be conscious. This is the materialism of Sartre; a materialism not in the sense that the physical 'explains' the spiritual (it is almost the reverse which is the case, as we shall see) but in the sense that the spiritual can no longer be looked upon as enjoying a semi-autonomy, as being capable of living within itself. One cannot 'reject' the world in favour of one's memories, feelings or thoughts, for these are exterior to subjectivity, they are ways in which it is possible to 'exist' the world, they are not a refuge from it.

Now while it is true that the for-itself *is* the perceived object (since there is consciousness of nothing else) it is equally true that we are conscious of not being the object concerned; but for this to be the case, the for-itself must identify the object which it is not, and the problem is, how can a 'nothingness' accomplish this. It is here that Sartre introduces his analysis of bad faith by which he demonstrates that the for-itself not only denies that it is a given object, but proposes itself as being something quite different. Man is an animal capable of the surprising feat of misleading *himself*, of sincerely denying concrete evidence that he is in love, a coward, a homosexual, etc., by asserting that he is as a matter of fact indifferent, courageous, attracted to women, etc. Consequently, the for-itself not only is not what it is, it is what it is not—it is the absent wealth of experience and knowledge which must in some way be present (it is 'present' as a nothingness) if a given thing is to be intelligible. The necessity of philosophical rigour makes what is quite simple appear complicated—all Sartre is saying is that there is no being without nothingness, no truth without falsehood, etc., but of course this platitude has taken on a new importance and meaning. Good and evil, for example, have no existence apart from consciousness, they are 'existed' by the for-itself which, however, cannot *be* good without at the same time not being it. The more 'honest' the woman, the greater her preoccupation with the looseness of her neighbours— the for-itself is what it is not.

The process we have been describing is what Sartre calls a 'nihilation'—the act by which the for-itself, obliged to identify precisely what it is conscious of not being, marshals those absent entities which constitute its particular world view into a 'muff' of nothingness surrounding that of which there is consciousness.

It has been emphasized from the beginning that subjectivity is not a thing but an 'intention', or purposeful act; and it is this aspect of the question that remains to be dealt with. What is the purpose of the 'nihilating' activity of the for-itself to which we owe the existence of the world as we know it?

We have seen that the for-itself both is and is not the perceived object. It is, in other words, at a distance from itself; it is necessarily separated from itself, since if it *were* the object (without at the same time not being it) there could be no consciousness. Nothing characterizes man more strongly than desire (even the fakir whose goal in life is the suppression of desire, desires at least that) and this is so because the whole effort of the for-itself is bent to the elimination of the division within itself. The for-itself seeks to 'coincide' with itself, which is another way of saying that the for-itself, which is a nothingness, desires the self-sufficient being of substance without ceasing to be consciousness. It seeks to realize a fusion of the object and that 'absent' world which makes it intelligible; to suppress the contingency of every perceived object (and hence of itself, since the for-itself *is* the object) by making it 'self intelligible'. If this could be achieved, our questions could cease, we should enjoy the peaceful plenitude of the fully explained, of the justified. The absurd, that perpetual menace of our honest and lucid moments, would be exorcised. But this is manifestly impossible since, as we have seen, there is no consciousness apart from the nihilating denial that the for-itself is the perceived object, and this separation at the heart of the for-itself could be suppressed only by the suppression of consciousness itself.

The above is a gross over-simplification of little more than a single chapter of *Being and Nothingness*, that entitled Immediate Structures of the For-itself, which, however, is probably the most difficult of the book.[1] But even though the reader has been unable to follow the argument in detail, he will be able to appreciate the way in which Sartre's philosophy (not, of course, in itself, but as part of a half-century of continental art and thought) makes it feasible for us to regard the world not as 'pre-existent' to man, but as constituted by human intentionality. We have seen that what the in-itself is, will depend upon the nature of that absent world which the for-itself calls into being in an attempt to identify that which it is conscious of not being. But this is simultaneously an effort on the part of the for-itself to be what it is not, it is literally a pro-ject, and it is this project (what we have been calling orientation, choice, intention, etc.) which

[1] Anglo-Saxon philosophers declare *Being and Nothingness* to be a simple exercise in the misuse of language (though they have begun to temper the condescension of a decade ago) and so betray again their persistent refusal to understand that philosophy is not an understanding of reality but in part a creation of it. Again the 'objective' monk is at one with the conservative society which employs him. For the conservative, society has reached an approximately definitive form; it is given, like the world of Anglo-Saxon philosophy.

in large measure determines the nature of our world. One who continued to worship in a church that had been turned into a gymnasium would be considered mad or at best eccentric; and yet such a person would have correctly perceived the building as a church. It is none the less a gymnasium, even with its appearance all but unchanged both inside and out. A mere 'nothing', a change of intention, has sufficed to alter the world. Similarly, it is not the past but the way in which we envisage the future which in large measure determines the present.

It will be recalled that we identified progress with the disintegration of belief in a world inexorably given, in which it was easy to regard men as products, as things, rather than as the sources of value. We have known for a century or so that man created God, we now see in what sense he may be said to create the world.[1] But if the world is not identifiable apart from our intentions in respect to it, then that intention constitutes us, as well as the world; or, as Sartre says, man invents himself each day. In classical thought, there is an exact repetition on the subjective level of what occurs when we consider the world around us; that is, just as we reason our way to an Absolute for which there is no evidence in consciousness, so the identification of ourselves as given things is a reasoned process to which we have recourse because we are conscious not of an enduring thing but only of a ceaselessly shifting sequence of things. For purposes of spiritual tranquillity, we 'construct' ourselves (as heroic, devout, honest, frank, etc.) precisely as the philosopher constructs a system with which to explain the exterior world. In a sense, we are back to Zeno's arrow which has to be 'stopped' to be made intelligible —in the same way we 'stop' the feverish activity which we *are*, because of this alone we are conscious, by manufacturing or receiving a fixed identity, that of an Aryan, a good American, a public school man, a cultivated gentleman, a virtuous woman, etc., an identity which will enable us to act in a given situation always in a given way, just as water always boils at a given temperature. The Frenchman who is a 'patriot' need not concern himself about Algeria—his conduct will be the automatic one of the impelled object. It is common enough to see in Kafka a literary anticipa-

---

[1] This does not mean that his freedom is so unrestricted that it is meaningless as Sartre's critics tirelessly insist. First, because consciousness is always of a specific or contingent thing; it is rooted to a given time and place, it is 'situated'; and secondly because we have to take into account the existence of other people.

tion of our conviction that philosophical and scientific system building is primarily the expression of a wish, not a revelation of 'reality'. It is natural, in our still monk-ridden culture, for it to be far less commonly recognized that Gide did for the 'inner world' precisely what Kafka did for the outer—he helped destroy an ancient faith in the virtue of introspection, which reached such a pitch of exacerbation in the romantics. We cannot 'know ourselves' for there is nothing to know, and the attempt is simply a device for 'stopping the arrow'. When introspection produces positive results we can be sure that the individual concerned is playing a role, just as the cultivated believer of the twentieth century is, in reality, simply making a desperate effort to believe.[1]

We can now return to the question of how Sartre has supplemented and developed marxism.

It is with Hegel that philosophy first tries to do something about rationalism's great mishap, the separation of mind and body. In rationalist thought, mind and matter are *related* in some way; Hegel shows how they may be considered to be at least interdependent, and this he achieves with the concept of alienation. Before there can be thought there must be consciousness, and consciousness of self is only achieved through 'desire', or 'alienation' in matter. To identify itself, consciousness must literally embody itself—somewhat the way in which a child may be looked upon as one great, diffuse or 'atomised' wish, which suddenly 'crystallizes', that is, identifies itself in this or that object. This process is an alienation in the sense that the thing is always an imperfect reflection of the self, which continues to 'search' for itself in the dialectic, and in so doing engenders history. But Hegel would not have been a nineteenth-century thinker had he not envisaged a happy ending, and in the philosophy of Hegel himself, consciousness finally comes to rest in the Idea, finally 'coincides' with itself. But this is a 'solution' which pertains exclusively to the realm of thought, and while Kierkegaard protested in the name of existence, only Marx was able to show how thought could be brought back into effective contact with existence. This he accomplished by redefining the concept of alienation in such a way as to reanimate the dialectic. Marx was helped in this by Feuerbach who pointed out

[1] There is still, to be sure, a certain amount of genuine faith, just as there was, no doubt, an occasional atheist even in the middle ages. We are interested, however, in social phenomena, and on this level, the Church is not primarily faith, but political reaction.

that it is not God (or the Idea) who alienates himself in man, but, on the contrary, man who alienates himself in God. In other words, alienation, properly considered, consists in depriving men of what they themselves have produced, whether this occurs through superstition, as in religion, or through social oppression as in capitalism. We shall not appreciate the force of this conception unless we bear in mind the Hegelian version of it; just as consciousness of self is only possible in and through objects, so the worker *is* what he produces, and to take away what he produces is to take away not only his food and clothing but the only legitimate means of identifying himself. Since the time of Marx, the worker has become a consumer; but this does not invalidate the marxian conception of alienation provided that, with the help of Hegel, we enlarge it somewhat. Everyone admits the 'soullessness' of modern industrial labour, but then they hasten to attribute it to the nature of modern production which makes it impossible for the worker to be responsible for the entire unit, or even part of a unit, since he is so often merely an assembler. But if the pre-industrial craftsman was not alienated in the sense in which we are using the word, it was not primarily because he had produced the entire and hence utilizable unit, but because he himself had determined in large measure precisely what it should be, in appearance, in quality, etc. He could consequently 'recognize himself' in the finished product, and what is therefore essential is not that a product issue from a man's own hands, but from his own will, which will always coincide more or less with the common will. The soullessness of modern industry is the result not of the division of labour, but of the fact that the nature of the goods produced is determined by the employer rather than the worker, and the goal of the employer is neither beauty nor utility, but profit—his is not part of the common will.

I suggested that what is new in the present situation, and what classical marxism must be developed to cope with, is the fact that the worker has consented to his alienation in exchange for the products of modern industry; indeed, he even aspires to it. He has accepted to be what he owns rather than what he does. What is saddest in this, is not that the worker should have taken the mess of pottage but that the intellectual should encourage him to do so. The decay of marxist thought has left the masses of the people more abandoned than they have ever been before. At one time, men who were unfit to earn a living in any other way could go into the army. There they were given

123

food and clothing on condition that they cease to exist as a personal will or intention, as a man, in other words; and the whole purpose of army drill is to make men look as much as possible like things. The modern industrial worker has done precisely that: sold his birthright for a standard of living.

We have seen in what sense man may be considered to be a 'nothingness'. He is not thing, but 'movement toward' things which are perpetually 'one jump ahead' since to 'overtake' (that is, to identify) is simultaneously to make that intentional projection without which the world falls into unintelligibility. Is not this endless search for an impossible fixed identity, for 'thinghood', precisely the alienation of which we are talking? Alienation in the philosophy of Sartre is the seeking of an identity through the appropriation of goods or culture (as possession). It is the attempt people make to justify their existence in terms of what they have acquired rather than in terms of what they have *done*. The for-itself is a nothingness, and the most effective means of denying this is to surround ourselves with objects which will proclaim the reverse. The man who lives in this fine house cannot be a nobody; the man who knows such eminent people must be somebody, etc., etc. To this day the bourgeois is struggling to wash away the disgrace of lowly birth, and his folk hero is the lad who rises from rags to riches. No one will enquire how the money was made, for the goal is to be, not to do. It is for this reason that the bourgeois' sole criterium for judging a man (though he will hypocritically allege others) is what he owns—hence the horror of marxism which in abolishing property abolishes morality. We have seen that truth is what we consent to take cognizance of, not what we painstakingly seek out; and does not the conservative slogan 'the socialist is someone who wants something for nothing' make it perfectly clear that for the conservative (who, ironically enough, is usually a better 'christian' than the worker) worldly goods, being life's most precious gift, the consecration of a life well spent, must be withheld from the unworthy? If there is no possibility, in this occidental 'free world' of *doing something*, then we can always *be somebody*, and to this end the worker will try to send his child to a public school and begin to vote conservative. He is obliged to alienate himself in the attempt *to be* for he has no idea what *to do*. Is not the goal of the labour party itself less to abolish class than to institute a universal middle class? A pretty prospect, and one that shows the country to be utterly without a real opposition. The only genuine opposition must

124

be moral, but as matters stand, the conservative morality of 'status through acquisition' is also that of the labour party which differs only in its generous conviction that the gates of respectability should be opened to the entire nation. This is not to say that the labour party consciously intends to universalize the horrors of middle-class 'culture', but that its affection for safe thinking (which is all the objective or non-thought of the universities has equipped it to carry out) is allowing it to happen.

Conservatism is the preposterously anachronistic attempt to equate social status with political authority, and when it takes up arms to defend its hoary ethic we call it fascism. The popular appeal of which fascism had need in its early phases, it acquires by extending status from money and birth to nationality—this simple device enables the masses to achieve a precise self-definition, it endows them with a place; in brief, it 'freezes' activities into things, it substitutes a definition for a constructive purpose; for when fascism is dynamic, it merely proclaims the 'rights' following from an arbitrary definition (the definition of the German race as 'superior' and consequently as having the right to dominate the world) rather than those following from an activity (Russia having *achieved* communism first, she has the right to lead other nations to a similar accomplishment). Communism resembles fascism to the degree in which it uses its ideology as an infallible means of distinguishing the 'good' from the 'bad' (as a means of defining) rather than as a programme. But there remains a fundamental difference: fascist determination comes 'from behind', that of communism 'from ahead'; in other words, fascism bases judgement upon what a man *is* (or is supposed to be), communism upon what he *does* (or is supposed to do). In the former we are dealing with a 'substance' or 'essence', in the latter with an act. To make this perfectly clear we need only contrast American with communist witch-hunting. In America, it is sufficient to have been a communist for two days in the thirties to bear the stain for ever, no amount of good americanism can ever wash it away. In communist countries, on the contrary, it is possible (at least in theory, and no doubt sometimes in practice) by an avowal of past errors and a promise of better conduct in the future, to be restored to favour. The communist condemns the bourgeois for what he does (he exploits the worker, etc.) but the fascist condemns the Jews, the negroes, the communists, the 'lower classes', etc. for what they are. During the painful years of Stalin's lifetime (with its tragic prolongation in the putting down of the Hungarian revolt), this distinction was difficult to bear in mind, but it was nevertheless making communism, despite its outrages, big with the future. The masses of Asia turn toward communism exactly as the masses of the ancient world turned toward christianity which opened its arms to that immense majority shut out from Roman citizenship or Greek culture, just as the asiatic was shut out from the possession of a white skin, or as, in this country, having a certain accent (the outward sign of an inward essence) is absolutely indispensable to true distinction. Fascism[1] is not a passing outbreak of collective 'irrationality', it is not merely capitalism defending itself, it is the rotting corpse of an entire culture; one which, for the historical reasons we have considered in previous chapters, holds man to be a thing with given characteristics rather than an act with given aims. 1789 was prepared by more than a century of re-evaluation. Not only does the Anglo-Saxon intellectual refuse to re-evaluate, he is capable of arguing that value judgements, being the mere 'expression of emotion' are not a legitimate object of philosophical enquiry. How easily one understands that men should turn in desperation to religion if 'thought' of this kind is to be the alternative.

---

[1] The fascism of the fifties is not, of course, identical with that of the thirties. It has taken the form of the 'father figure' and, so far at least, has been relatively benign. The elevation of men like Churchill, Eisenhower, De Gaulle, Nasser, Nkrumah, Nehru (and now the curious campaign to glamourize Macmillan), indicates that the cultural and intellectual abdication of the 'free world' has opened the way not to pluralism, but to the increasing dependence of law upon men over law. In communism, the politician is subordinate to doctrine, and while the doctrine can be oppressive it does not at least lead sooner or later to anarchy.

126

CONCLUSION

W HEN Alain said that 'to think is to invent without believing', he neatly defined rationalist thought in its death throes. But there remains dialectical thought which, after having been eclipsed for almost a century by that aggravated form of rationalism we call scientism, is now coming into its own. If we can no longer believe in thought as the revelation of a 'pre-existent' reality, if we are to be aware that thinking is 'invention'; that is, if we cannot believe in it as an explanation, we can nevertheless believe in it as an anticipation of the real, as a tool with which to bring the actual abreast of the possible. In classical rationalism, as we have seen, mind is merely related to matter, there can therefore be no question of a creative thought in the literal sense; and although Hegel showed mind and matter to be interdependent, matter had, for that very reason, to take on a rationality (as in dialectical materialism) that our modern experience has been unable to confirm. A solution may be worked out if we move down to a level beneath that of the intellect and the 'I', to that of consciousness which (as in the for-itself of Sartre) may be regarded as, at one and the same time, receiving and constituting reality. In this way, historical rationality may be retained since it is human intentionality which constitutes the real; and yet for that very reason, this is a real which can never be posed as an Absolute.

It is true, as Saint Augustine held, that one must believe in order to know, except that belief, for us, must be belief in the creative possibilities of man's social projects. Here in the west the objective intellectual has *created* a totally meaningless historical situation by declining to entertain a project for his society. He has placed himself in the absurd position of having to contemplate a finished work, knowing full well that history admits of no such monstrosity.

To rob our society of its future, to make it meaningless, is at the same time to universalize bourgeois culture, since the only project left to the worker is to better his standard of living. Once basic needs are taken care of, this becomes a race for respectability; but while respectability was of vital importance for the bourgeoisie (because of the conflict between theory and practice which we have discussed), for the worker it fulfils no function whatever, and he therefore alienates himself far more disastrously than did the bourgeois. It is a commonplace that classical rationalism is the intellectual instrument of middle-class rule; but we have also seen that this rationalism assumes the existence of subjectivity considered as a thing, as a self which it is one of the functions of culture as possession to 'ennoble', much as the Italian renaissance tyrant attempted to put a good face upon his seizure of power by attaching to his court not buffoons, a luxury which only legitimacy could allow itself, but poets and artists. What we must understand is that this ideal of a self capable of living on its own provisions[1] is not one of the elements of bourgeois civilization which we must try to retain (since, as we have seen, it is not inseparable from political freedom); on the contrary, it is a serious obstacle to the birth of a culture in which the mass of the people could share. One has the impression that if it were not for the 'educated', modern art would be far more widely appreciated than it is. The majority of the people are, at worst, indifferent or amused; open hostility is left to those with a pretence to culture. In this respect Epstein's autobiography is a decisive document.

A culture is a looking-glass in which the dominant social group seeks its features; and the astonishing thing about the bourgeoisie is that it is compelled to use the mirrors of by-gone cultures, since its own great artists have generally refused to take it seriously. One need only think of Victorian architecture, consisting entirely of clumsily borrowed styles; of the fondness for classical studies, renaissance art, the study of history, etc. The fact that today our rulers are as indifferent to these values as are the 'lower orders' proves simply that the bourgeoisie has given up all pretence of legitimatizing its domination and now founds it upon open force as in fascism, or conceals it behind the current myth (countenanced by the labour party leaders)

[1] In this connection, one should bear in mind the terrible loneliness which modern communities inflict upon many thousands of their members.

of an industry rendered beneficent by the 'separation of ownership and control'. What has really happened is the evolution of the entrepreneur into an anonymous member of a closely-knit power élite. The universities are, of course, well behind this development, and are still providing culture for the relatively receptive nineteenth-century gentleman who has given way to the vulgar *fêtard* of the modern privileged classes.

If we are to do anything about this situation it should be recognized that a successful revolution must be cultural as well as political.[1] If the people are to govern themselves, in other words if direct communication between rulers and ruled is to be maintained, then the rulers must be regarded as different in function, not different in status. But this will require an entire cultural reorientation based upon a conception of man as act and not substance. In stalinism, communication is ineffective because it takes place indirectly by way of the dogma—the rulers become despositories of the Truth (things), rather than participants in a common effort (acts). In the west, communication breaks down because culture is not functional, it either confers status or aims at the creation of self-contained individuals who, not wishing to be subjectivities with the basic and 'common' human needs, can only communicate through a body of culture which is for the most part unwieldy, irrelevant and, in any case, designed for other purposes.

One needs to know university life at first hand to be aware of the fearful intellectual apathy in both staff and students produced by the notion of learning as the fabricator of a superior self rather than as a tool. This essentially 'aristocratic' conception which professes to combat the cretinizing effects of newspaper, television, and so on, actually works in precisely the same way as do the 'mass media'. The students, who come to the university to be 'filled up', and who refuse to make the slightest intellectual effort on their own behalf, are perfectly aware of this. Any attempt on their part to utilize the facts at their disposal, or simply to react in some practical way would be after all contrary to the practice of their teachers. But the 'self-organizing' facts of which consists the quaint universe of the monk and which the student need simply absorb, passively, do not create

[1] In the Russia of 1917, marxism was precisely that. But in the west, marxism (as a 'scientism') remained part of classical rationalism which had already produced its revolution. This is perhaps the best explanation for the perpetual betrayals of European socialism.

cultivated individuals leading lives on a higher plane than their fellows. They give rise to semi-literate masses who have advanced one step further towards respectability; one step further towards alienation in the sense that they have been equipped with an additional means of self-identification, an additional means of shielding from themselves the knowledge that they are only in so far as they do. It has become the practice for anyone wishing to condemn socialism to point to the hideous example of Russia. One therefore feels free to recall that in America, the land of the future, our western university education has produced not 'individuals' fighting to protect their priceless heritage of free thought, but precisely the opposite—the so-called 'organization man'. This is a man who actually aspires to the commonly shared stupidity, who dreads nothing more than distinguishing himself by independent thought, whose only ideal is to conform as closely as possible to the dictates of his group. This is animal farm with a vengeance. The Hungarians, at least, reached the point where they would accept no more; but can we hope for a revolt of the organization man, the modern eunuch who, in exchange for a superb standard of living, delightedly mutilates himself?

This is the most frightening aspect of present-day western culture —it has developed a form of alienation to which the people consent. Where are we to place responsibility for such a situation if not squarely on the shoulders of the academics and more especially the philosophers whose function it is, as Nietzsche remarked, to be creators of value? In the past, opposition came from the learned and intelligent members of the leisured classes or from the suffering in the streets. Today, there is neither a responsible leisured class nor serious physical privation; there are only the universities which have become closed and self-perpetuating systems. The arts faculties of our universities are engaged exclusively in training suitable students to fill its vacancies, and the only suitable ones are those predisposed to look upon the academic not as a dedicated servant of his society but as one of its adornments.[1] I recently attended a history lecture in the course of which the teacher explained to his students that scientific

[1] If the academic does not feel the tyranny involved here, it is because he has nothing whatever to say against the system. The communist teacher who accepts communism as fully as the western academic accepts his own set of values is as free as anyone in the west; while one of our teachers who undertook to attack the whole ethic of objectivity with the sense of urgency which the circumstances demand would become a pariah.

investigation had for the first time become a moral problem, scientists having to bear in mind the frightful consequences that could follow from the abuse of the immense power they were placing in men's hands. Apart from the silliness of supposing that a scientist, or anyone else, would refuse to know something that was waiting to be known, we have here a clear expression of the academic's refusal to accept responsibility for anything, his function being to adorn; to be objective, as he calls it. The fault therefore will always lie with the scientist or the politician.

A university career is the noblest of all because it should be that of the guide, the counsellor, the creator of values. But it is also the most exacting because we no longer believe that values are discovered, we know them to be created, and they will consequently change from one historical context to another, in part even from one generation to another.

In considering the present historical situation, the job of the academic appears clear. While fascism is dormant, we must seize the opportunity to kill it. We must face squarely the fact that the technical lead over the west which Russia now enjoys is one aspect of an *ideological lead*, which between the Declaration of Independence and the advent of marxism was held by America. Whatever the crimes of communism, there is no doubt but what it represents a historical advance, and the a-historical 'thinking' of western intellectuals exists for the purpose of blinding us to that simple fact. But since communism represents, historically, a more advanced system than our own, there can be no question of its ever accepting *our* terms, and the one hope for permanent peace lies in our willingness to take up marxism once again at the point where it went astray into scientism.

The work is well under way in France. Sartre, like Marx, regards his philosophy as a tool; and, as I have tried to show by arguing that modern art, like Sartre's existentialism, is at once a constitution and an understanding of reality, Sartre, like Marx, is firmly embedded in his time—an excellent guarantee of the effectiveness of the tool he is forging. Inversely, the incredible triviality of Anglo-Saxon philosophy may be attributed in part to the fact that the logical positivism[1]

---

[1] Technically speaking, the positivist experiment has ceased to interest British philosophers. But its spirit is in no way diminished. Logical positivism came into being as a reaction against idealism which had a tendency to take words for things. The positivists insisted that propositions should be susceptible to correlation with fact, and they dreamed of working out a system which would guarantee that this was always done. In this way philosophy could at last be converted into

with which most of it is related, was already outdated before the first world war, with the appearance of such books as Meyerson's *Identité et Réalité* and, of course, the early work of Husserl. In fact, we can go back still further, to 1874, the year in which appeared Boutroux's book *De la Contingence des Lois de la Nature*, in which he makes the following remark: 'For as long as we deal with reflex actions we are concerned with things known, not with knowing persons.' Now, only the 'scientific' philosopher could suppose a philosophy capable of dissociating itself from its age; for everyone else, every philosophy is part of a given cultural structure (what Goldmann calls a 'world view') and, furthermore, the best understanding of it is to be achieved through a study of its role within a given world view rather than its role in the history of philosophy. With the help of Boutroux's remark, I think we may throw light on the relationship between the philosophies of positivism and the politics of our present society. In classical rationalism (to which all present-day Anglo-Saxon thinking is still tributary) mind is a kind of 'reflex action' stimulated by 'things known' and not by the 'knowing person'. In this philosophy, subjectivity (or the 'knowing person') is an *aberration*; man is an object, a classifier of things known. However repulsive the idea may appear, fascism can be shown to be an outgrowth of 'objective' bourgeois philosophy as well as of bourgeois government and economics, inasmuch as fascism, as we have seen, is simply an extreme development of the notion of man as object.

Sartre is therefore fully justified in looking upon his philosophy as

an exact science. At first sight linguistic philosophy rids us of so naïve a scientism by declaring that there are no final solutions in philosophy for the simple reason that there are no problems. All problems are false problems created by the careless use of language which, meaningful and accurate as a tool for daily living, gives trouble only when utilized to more speculative ends. What made logical positivism a positivism in the nineteenth-century sense was not only its belief in solutions to philosophical problems, but also its deeper lying presupposition of a world in which facts exist independently of our awareness of them—the 'ready-made' world I have referred to. The logical positivist's strong dislike for metaphysics can only be justified if he assumes a 'pre-constituted' world which metaphysical speculation obscures, and which will only be illuminated by patient research. All this is true of linguistic philosophy except that the methodology of logical positivism is now without a constructive purpose. Let it not be supposed that this is a remark to which a linguistic philosopher might take exception. In an article entitled 'Analysis and Imagination' published in *The Revolution in Philosophy* (Macmillan, 1956) we read: 'If one is told that it [the systematic study of language] serves no practical purpose, what can one do but say "No, of course not".' This, surely, is the fag-end of a culture.

a humanism, because it assigns a vital function to the 'knowing person', to subjectivity, which is neither aberrant nor irrational, but constitutive of the real. Anglo-Saxon philosophy is no longer a quest for the truth, it is a vested interest. It is protecting academic life from the intrusion of this catastrophic idea—knowledge is not received, it is made. Knowledge as possession excludes human intercourse (and this applies, thanks to specialization, even to the learned), knowledge as intention, restores it. The 'intention' of the inhabitants of a town to remain behind and try to save their homes from rising waters creates a situation in which the individual draws strength from the group (since alone he would be powerless to act) and the group from the individual (since the individual helps to *constitute* the town as one to be saved and not abandoned).

It is this dialectic between occurrences and the objective meaning which man's subjective intentions attach to them that makes historical movement. It is the job of the academic to see that these intentions are at once sufficiently inspiring and sufficiently practical to give our lives a meaning entirely apart from reference to status and possession. This is something that the reformism of people like Karl Popper can never do; for what it gives with one hand, such as improvements in standards of living, it takes back with the other by allowing the accumulation of historical refuse such as social castes. We have had a century in which to recognize the futility of reformism, which only accomplished as much as it did thanks to the existence of a well-defined political philosophy in irreducible opposition to the one prevailing. What, therefore, is to be hoped from a reformism priding itself upon a 'refutation' of marxism?

INDEX